Don Da Grade

Maintenance and Repair of Band Instruments

FOR BAND DIRECTORS AND INSTRUMENTALISTS

Maintenance and Repair of Band Instruments

For Band Directors and Instrumentalists

by

George H. Springer

ALLYN and BACON, Inc. Boston

ACKNOWLEDGEMENTS

I extend my sincere appreciation to: B. A. Nugent, Albert Fitzgerrel, David Salsbury, Theresa Turley, Esther Stegemann, James Fleisher, and Edmund C. Williams.

Library of Congress Card Number: 76-118036

Printed in the United States of America

Contents

Preface

During my eleventh year as a band director, I was asked by a repairman-friend if I would like to learn the repair business. After accepting, I spent the next three and one-half years as owner of a repair shop where I learned what I should have known as a band director—the necessity of systematic care and maintenance of wind instruments and a familiarity with standard repair practices.

In serving instrumentalists of all levels of proficiency, I came to realize that an unnecessary barrier exists between many directors and repairmen, a semantic barrier of misunderstanding created by the use of non-standard terminology. An "overhaul" to some means "a checking over;" others refer to "overhaul" when desiring only a "repad;" and some repairmen, not interpreting the customer's instructions correctly, will perform a "playing condition" repair when a "repad" was desired.

Urged by band directors to write a repair manual, and remembering my own repair problems as a director, I have tried to make a positive contribution to music education by presenting a realistic approach to band instrument repair problems and to eliminate misunderstandings by including a chapter on terminology.

Montalba, Texas   **George H. Springer**

Maintenance
and Repair of
Band Instruments

FOR BAND DIRECTORS AND INSTRUMENTALISTS

Introduction

One of the side benefits of attending a music convention is the discovery that all band directors have similar problems. When large assemblies are dismissed and dissolve into the small intimate groups that invariably dot the convention center lobby, the conversation often turns to the ludicrous accidents that occasionally befall each director. If one of the stories concerns the twisting of a neckpipe, the breaking of braces, or the warping of tuning slides, most of the experienced directors in the circle will nod with understanding.

Repairmen, too, have their stories and share mutual experiences. One story that is often told concerns a customer who drove over 100 miles to get an expensive saxophone repaired for a forthcoming program, only to discover that the inoperative G♯ key was caused by an unhooked spring.

Although every band director cannot be a proficient repairman, he can and should learn a few basic facts and techniques that will save many thousands of lost student-hours in music education each year. When *all* students play instruments in good condition, every aspect of musicianship will improve.

Many repairmen are ex-directors or professional musicians who often understand the director's problems better than the director understands the repair business. Time is the repairman's salary. Show respect for his salary and you will probably never need to complain about his service.

If, on the other hand, the repairman fails consistently to meet the promised date for repairs and is careless in his work, he is not showing respect for the customer's obligations and should not be considered for future business.

A review of repair manuals, care and maintenance pamphlets, and repair chapters in music education textbooks reveals one of the reasons why band directors and instrumentalists are often weak in this phase of their profession. Following are some of the findings in repair literature.

1. Some repair practices which are presented to the novice as standard procedures are of a questionable nature.

2. Sometimes identical or similar illustrations and procedures are given for several instrument repairs when one presentation would suffice.

3. A maze of details and illustrations, unnecessary for even the novice, often accompanies simple procedures.

4. The "knack" of using makeshift equipment is, seemingly, given more emphasis than proper repair procedures.

5. Some texts refer simple problems to the repair shop. With no instructions available, instrumentalists in remote areas must "experiment" or lose valuable time by shipping the instrument to a repairman.

6. Accurate information prepared by expert repairmen is often too general, too limited in scope, or too advanced for many directors and instrumentalists.

An attempt has been made in this book to eliminate duplication by first presenting procedures that are common to several instruments, followed by instructions pertaining to specific instruments. The solution to each repair problem is given in a step by step approach which is intended to be brief and concise.

In addition to the Table of Contents and the Index, the text is organized to aid the reader in locating a subject by heading. After the chapter heading is the first large division, Brass, followed by a smaller subdivision, French Horn, and a side heading for specific problems, Repairing Stuck Valves. Many illustrations are given to clarify the instructions. Asterisks follow words which are identified in the "Terminology" chapter.

This book is based upon the writer's personal experiences during ten years as a band director in the public schools (grades 4 through 12), and on experience gained in more than three years as the owner of a repair shop in Dallas, Texas, where he served both amateur and professional musicians.

1

Care and Maintenance

Thousands of dollars are spent each year by instrument manufacturers on free literature to aid the band director in discharging his duties. But this literature can be of no benefit unless properly used. Included in such publications are care and maintenance pamphlets which can assist in the elimination of many annoying repair problems.

Though the frequency of presentation will vary according to the method used, proper care of instruments should be taught as faithfully as any aspect of music instruction.

Instrument inspection is often one of the requirements in marching contests and the director must conform to whatever military style procedures are customary in his region. It is doubtful, however, if a "by the numbers" inspection, even though impressive, can be as effective as an examination by a conscientious director who is thoroughly familiar with good care and maintenance practices.

Although many directors have eliminated the following problems, others may discover tips that will help them prevent future liabilities.

GENERAL PRECAUTIONS

Damage to instruments is most frequently caused by inexperienced handling. Unless it is part of a definite teaching program, students should not play each other's instruments!

Cases should be kept as near as possible to performance areas. All instruments should be placed in cases when not in the students' own hands. Even if attendants are present in a partitioned band section of the bleachers during the third quarter break, seat vibrations from an adjoining section of the bleachers or an excited youngster racing through the band section can cause damage to un-cased instruments. Having the case nearby also helps if a sudden rainstorm should occur.

Thoughtful planning is needed in storing instruments such as the sousaphone, or percussion and mallet instruments. The urge to "bang" on the percussion instruments or throw trash in the sousaphones is a normal tendency of human behavior. A shortage of storage space need be no problem. A hinged, four-sided box of ⅛-inch fibreboard can be easily constructed to cover the tympani, marimba, etc., when not being used. Sousaphones and glockenspiels can be suspended from wall hooks just above the players' chairs, and sousaphone bell covers can be made of cheesecloth with an elastic edge for easy removal. Most teachers of home economics will assist in the design of attractive covers with school initials, etc., for use in half-time shows.

Poorly designed instrument lockers that necessitate stacking, crowding or storing in unconventional positions; lockers located near exits or in congested hallways; and storage rooms with only one door contribute to instrument damage. If such a situation exists and cannot be remedied, rehearsals should be ended a few minutes early in order to prevent the frantic last minute rush for lockers. An early dismissal also allows time for proper woodwind swabbing.

The band trip is another cause of instrument damage. Warped trombone slides, dented sousaphones, and broken drum heads frequently result from hasty loadings. Packing quilts can be purchased for a fraction of the cost of bass drum heads and major repairs on sousaphones. Careful loading by a dependable band manager can prevent damage to all of the instruments.

Eating candy, chewing gum, and drinking carbonated beverages just before (or while) playing can cause dirty mouthpieces, sticking pads, sluggish valves, corroded slides and poor intonation. This often occurs during the third quarter break. Though the director cannot deny his students a period of relaxation, he can and should develop some practical means of alleviating this problem.

IMPORTANCE OF THE CASE

The importance of a good instrument case had been overlooked by nearly everyone except the zealous musician and manufacturer. From the days when the cardboard case, the drawstring sack, the "doc's bag," or the "smuggler's case" could be purchased for a few dollars comes the mistaken idea that a new trumpet case costing twenty per cent as much as a student trumpet is the best made. Despite its sturdy appearance, it is usually constructed of specially treated cardboard which is no thicker than a hardback book cover. However, such a case may be adequate if the instrument fits properly, the straps or turnbuttons* adjust snugly, and the case latches function correctly. Too often when a student fails to fasten the instrument after placing it in the case, the lid will unexpectedly open (due to a faulty latch) and the instrument will fall out. A dollar's worth of materials and a few minutes of time can often prevent such mishaps.

*See Chapter 6, "Terminology"

A student who refuses to have a faulty case latch replaced by the luggage shop repairman because it does not match the old one—or the student who intends to wait until he can find just the right shade of velvet before he replaces the broken turnbutton—is only inviting trouble.

Loose articles (valve oil, lyres, mouthpieces, key oil, cork grease, screw drivers, pliers, case deodorizers, reed clippers, swabs, atomizers, ligatures, mouthpiece caps, etc.) inside the case will eventually cause damage. Small, unsightly dents in brass instruments, including the valve casings*, are the result of failure to place accessories in the accessory compartment. Bent keys, chipped tone holes, and torn pad skins are casualties that plague the careless woodwind player. The saxophonist who is indifferent to loose articles will ultimately find that the "stuffy" sound his instrument has suddenly acquired is caused by a ligature or mouthpiece cap that has become lodged inside the upper body. If a case does not have an accessory compartment, a homemade drawstring sack will be sufficient.

The woodwind player who allows rubber bands, bits and pieces of cork, chamois, sponge rubber, chewing gum wrappers, old reeds, and lunch money to accumulate inside the case is sure to visit the repair shop needlessly. Stopped up tone holes and inoperative keys are the most frequent consequences of an untidy case.

Gym shorts, tennis shoes, folding music racks, bulky method books, and sack lunches, crowded in the case, are other causes of instrument damage. No case, however strong, can prevent impairment of the instrument if this practice is followed.

Although aesthetically poor, a case handle made of baling wire or a wire coat hanger covered with tape is safer than a weakly constructed or worn out handle. Damage can occur when a cased instrument is dropped from only waist height. The bicycle-riding bandsman who slips the case handle over the handle bars is following a dangerous practice. Much more serious than the damage to the instrument is the possibility of body injuries caused from hard bumps or sudden turns, since the instrument can become wedged between the front wheel and frame and send the student sprawling.

Even after every precaution has been taken by the director and students, the instrument will sometimes be involved in unavoidable accidents. The best insurance against damage is a sturdy case that is properly fitted to the instrument and *securely fastened inside.*

WOODWINDS

Swabbing

One of the most important items of woodwind care is the routine of *careful* swabbing after playing. Though there is disagreement among musicians as to whether moisture causes wood instruments to crack, keeping instruments free of moisture will not only eliminate that possibility but will prevent a build-up of grime inside the bore—a major factor in intonation problems.

The turkey feather has been the traditional oboe swab for many years, but it is becoming less frequently used due to lack of availability and to the development of commercial swabs that will dry more thoroughly. One such swab is a soft, vinyl-covered cable with a small sponge that can be drawn completely through the upper joint.

Bassoon, clarinet, flute, piccolo, and saxophone swabs are available for drying all parts of the instruments and *should be used diligently.*

Bore Oiling

There is also controversy over the necessity for oiling the bores of wood instruments, but a careful, periodic oiling will do no harm and might possibly prevent cracking. The following steps should be observed:

1. Allow at least one day's drying time before oiling.
2. Select a good bore oil, olive oil, or almond oil.
3. Use a clean cloth or chamois swab with a few drops of oil and draw through the bore several times. To prevent excessive oil from soaking pads, insert a piece of wax paper under each of the closed key pads.
4. Let dry overnight if possible.

Here again, opinions vary widely on the frequency of oiling. Some believe that the new instrument should be oiled twice a week, while others feel that once a month is sufficient. The safest course to follow is the one recommended by the manufacturer or dealer to whom the instrument will be sent for adjustment if it should crack within the warranty period. The following schedule for oiling will be acceptable to most: once a week for the first two months, once a month for the next ten months and every six months thereafter. Whatever oiling frequency a director may choose for his teaching of care and maintenance, it is most important that he be consistent if he expects the students to follow his instruction.

Since the upper joints on most bassoons are treated with moisture resisting agents and the boot joint is rubber (or metal) lined, the bores should not be oiled unless so specified by the manufacturer.

Temperature and Humidity

Most pamphlets on woodwind care contain a warning against tempera-ture extremes, but the repairman must still occasionally pin* or band* a wood instrument which has been placed in a refrigerator or oven by a student who was trying to shrink a stuck tenon.* Cold instruments should be warmed gradually at room temperature before playing. Setting the instrument near a fireplace, radiator, or furnace vent is not advisable! Sudden changes of humidity should also be avoided if possible.

Key Oiling

A thorough oiling of metal hinge and pivot points and on saxophone key rollers once a month will assure smooth operation of keys and prevent formation of rust from perspiration acids. A key oil with a thin wire attached to the bottle cap is the most convenient to use, since it releases only a small drop of oil wherever its tip is placed. Care must be taken to prevent excessive oil from collecting around posts and from saturating the pads. Pipe cleaners can be used for absorbing excessive oil around the posts and in places difficult to reach with a cloth. A small artist's brush is a good accessory for removing the accumulation of dust around keys and posts.

Tone Holes

The accumulation of dirt and grime in the tone holes of oboes and clarinets is especially common. Since the application of only one thin coat of tuning oil* on a tone hole will "flatten" that note, the coating of several tone holes with dirt makes proper intonation impossible. By using a pipe cleaner or cotton swab, the player can keep the tone holes clean with very little effort.

Tenons

Dryness is the most common cause of loose or frayed tenon corks. Cork grease can be purchased at most any music store or repair shop and should be used periodically to keep the cork "live," and to allow ease in assembling. Mutton tallow* may be used as a satisfactory substitute for cork grease.

Broken tenons and warped keys are often the results of the pressure caused by the necessity of gripping the woodwind joint too tightly while assembling. If excessive pressure is caused by a moisture saturated, swelled tenon rather than a dry cork, consult the "Standard Repairs" chapter for procedures.

Improper care is another cause of chipped, worn, or broken tenons. The middle tenons of the clarinet and oboe, the foot tenon on the flute, and the tenor joint on the bassoon are points of unavoidable, structural weakness. Dropping or bumping assembled instruments will often cause expensive or irreparable damage. Laying an assembled woodwind instrument on a bed or in a chair is inviting disaster. Unsuspecting persons may accidentally sit on instruments which have been carelessly covered by an article of clothing, or a sheet or bedspread. Carelessness by a band member in passing through a door with a strong door closer is also responsible for occasional tenon damage to the assembled instrument.

Though some instrument manufacturers do not provide tenon caps* for the new instruments, caps may be purchased separately from music stores or repair shops. Not only does the tenon cap offer protection from breaking or chipping, it prevents accumulation of dust and trash on the greased tenon and discoloration of the case lining.

Particularly desirable are oboe tenon caps with felt washers that have been saturated with almond oil to prevent cracking. Players who have used them attest to their effectiveness.

The tenon that has become worn through long usage and allows leakage or looseness (despite the application of a new, thicker tenon cork) should be sent to the repair shop for installation of tenon caps (or shims).

Octave Tube

The octave tube*, inserted through the body of most woodwinds at the octave (or register) key, extends into the bore* to prevent water from entering the hole. This tube may become clogged occasionally by a particle from the swab. A broom straw or small, soft wire may be used to free the obstruction without removing the key. This opening is exceptionally critical, especially on the bassoon nib* and should not be cleaned with hard metal objects that will enlarge the hole. Accumulated water may be removed from octave tubes on smaller instruments by blowing air through the upper joint while closing all openings except the octave or register key. A common desk blotter can be a valuable asset for instruments that are prone to accumulate excessive amounts of water.

For more serious problems involving the octave tube*, consult the "Standard Repairs" chapter.

Mouthpiece

Three out of four clarinet and saxophone mouthpieces must be acid cleaned to remove the accumulated deposits caused by improper cleaning. The resonating chamber* of a woodwind mouthpiece is as sensitive as the resonating chamber on a fine violin and should be kept free of obstructions.

When played daily, clarinet and saxophone mouthpieces should be cleaned at least *once a week;* otherwise, saliva acids will cause chalky deposits that cannot be removed with soap and water.

A mouthpiece brush may be used, but care must be exercised when applying the brush to avoid scratching of the mouthpiece parts. It is safer to use a soft cloth with *luke-warm* water and bland soap. Since both plastic and hard rubber mouthpieces are susceptible to heat warpage, they *should not be cleaned in hot water!*

Mouthpieces of good quality can be restored to useable condition, even though they have been warped or contain deposits that cannot be removed with bland soap. These problems are covered in the "Standard Repairs" chapter.

Saxophone End Plugs

Like the tenon cap*, the end plug* is essential for protecting the instrument while it is in the case. A major cause of damage to the alto and tenor saxophone octave mechanisms is the failure of the player to insert the end plug before placing the saxophone in the case. The octave bridge* on most alto and tenor saxophones extends beyond the tenon receiver* and is made of soft brass. The slightest bump will often throw the automatic octave mechanism out of adjustment if it has been placed in the case without an end plug.

Saxophone octave problems which cannot be corrected by the band director should be brought to the attention of an experienced repairman.

Saxophone Drying

The saxophone is, without question, the most poorly cared for instrument in the woodwind family. Unsanitary deposits are found in a majority of saxophones from the neckpipe* to the bell bow*. Saliva accumulations are responsible for dried out (and leaking) pads, poor intonation, and tor pads whose skins have been eaten away by acids.

The construction of saxophones varies somewhat, but the pads which collect moisture on most saxophones are the low D♯ (E♭), the palm keys*, and the G♯. Thorough swabbing will alleviate the pad soaking which normally results if a saxophone is put in the case "wet." The application of neatsfoot oil to the affected pads will eliminate saturation of the pads while in playing position. It also keeps the pads supple, and it will assure longer service.

Cleaning the Neckpipe and Bocal*

If the director has been negligent in maintaining proper instrument care, he will find that the saxophone neckpipes and bassoon bocals contain accumulated grime and require special cleaning. After removing the octave key on the saxophone neckpipe, place it and the bocal in luke-warm, soapy water. Let them soak. A flexible brush (available at music stores) may be utilized for further cleaning of the saxophone neckpipe. A long, joined section of pipe cleaners and numerous "flushings" of the bassoon bocal will be necessary to remove the accumulations.

Since the bassoon bocal cannot be effectively swabbed after each playing, a weekly washing is necessary to keep its bore* free of dirt. Swabbing the saxophone neckpipe after each playing will eliminate the need for a periodic scrubbing.

Protecting the Finish

Acids from the human body are damaging to an instrument, even though it may have the new "epoxy" type lacquer, nickel plated keys, or a body and keys made of unplated silver. Continued handling can eventually tarnish or wear any material, but the destructive action of body chemicals can be slowed significantly if the player will carefully wipe fingerprints and saliva from the body and keys after each playing. A variety of wipe cloths, containing special chemicals for counteracting body acids on lacquer and silver instruments, is available from most music dealers. Conscientious use of these cloths will preserve the finish.

BRASS

General Remarks

Despite the fact that "care and maintenance" instructions contain adequate cleaning tips for brass instruments, the repairman frequently has to tell a customer that he needs a new mouthpipe. The first indication of this problem is the appearance of small, pink spots under the lacquer. These spots will soon develop into irreparable leaks. A new factory mouthpipe* that is properly installed, polished, and lacquered, will range in cost from ten to twenty-five per cent of the price of the instrument, depending on the brand and type. This is an expense that can be eliminated by proper care.

Piston Valve Instrument Cleaning

When a brass instrument is played daily, it should be thoroughly washed in warm, soapy water, with the valves removed and all slides pulled, *at least every two weeks.* During each washing, the mouthpipe should be cleaned with a flexible brush to remove the deposits to which it is most susceptible. The flexible brush should also be used on tubings and around the valve knuckles* where a greenish corrosion often appears. Care must be observed when cleaning around the valve casings* to prevent the scoring of valve walls and the formation of burrs which will hinder valve action.

Pistons should be carefully soaked in a separate container to prevent dents and scratches from contact with other metal parts. The walls of ports* are delicate and should be gingerly cleaned with a soft brush to remove the film that invariably forms there.

Trombone Cleaning

Flexible brushes are available for reaching the hand slide bow*, but there is danger in scratching the bearing surface with the metal parts of the brush. Unless the slide bow has deposits that need to be removed, only the rigid trombone cleaning rod should be used for cleaning the inside walls of the hand slide. The rod should be completely covered with a cloth so that no metal part can touch the walls. Enough surplus cloth should be left extending over the handle so that it can be firmly grasped to prevent its becoming lodged inside the tubing.

It is recommended by most manufacturers that the inside slides be cleaned with a weighted cord and cloth similar to the type used in clarinet cleaning, since the inside walls are more delicate than the outer slide. The outer surface of the inner slides should be cleaned with a clean cloth dampened by a non-abrasive liquid, such as kerosene. The use of wood alcohol or lacquer thinner should be avoided, since a drop of these liquids will damage some lacquer finishes. Unless the stockings* have troublesome deposits that cannot be removed by a non-abrasive compound, the director should not allow them to be buffed by a repairman. These stockings have been precision fitted to allow easy slide operation with a minimum of leakage. Buffing by harsh abrasives will remove valuable plating and destroy the snug fit.

Only the slide being cleaned must be held while cleaning. Otherwise, a warped slide may result.

Often overlooked in trombone cleaning are the cork barrels*. Dirt left inside the barrels will eventually work down to the slide surfaces and cause trouble. Feathers, pipe cleaners, small paint brushes or water under pressure can be utilized for cleaning this area.

The tuning slide and the tubing on trombones with the F attachment may be cleaned with a flexible brush in the same manner as the piston valve instruments.

Rotary Valve Instruments

The mouthpipe* of the French horn is more susceptible to acid damage than that of any other instrument and should be washed down and swabbed at least every two weeks. Some horns have a tuning slide on the end of the mouthpipe which will allow the flexible brush to pass completely through, thereby pushing the deposits outside. On horns whose mouthpipe connects to tubing which leads to a valve, the valve must be removed (see Figure 81, page 105), the flexible rod inserted as far as possible, and the mouthpipe flushed with water under pressure.

If the mouthpipe is cleaned consistently, a thorough "bathtub" cleaning, with all slides pulled and all valves removed, will be necessary only two or three times a year. At such times, the rotary valves*, the stems*, and the bearing washers* should be scrubbed and oiled. To prevent future trouble, the valves should be re-strung with new cord (see Figure 78, page 103).

Between cleaning periods, a thorough flushing of rotary valves with kerosene, lighter fluid, or penetrating oil will remove the saliva residue that can build up around the bearing surfaces and prevent valve oil from reaching the critical points. Flushing is especially effective for new instruments whose bearing tolerances are extremely small.

Sousaphone and Tuba Cleaning

The sousaphone, like the French horn, cannot be cleaned as easily as the smaller, piston valve instruments. However, the director can see that the valves are removed and cleaned and that the mouthpipe*, tuning bits*, and gooseneck* are scrubbed frequently. The necessity of diligence in such cleaning is evidenced by the filmy build-up in the valve ports, and the necessity for frequent replacement of the gooseneck and mouthpipe.

Unless the band director is fortunate enough to have school facilities that can accommodate tuba and sousaphone cleanings, it is more practical to have these instruments cleaned once a year in a repair shop.

Some directors have their tuba players use the garden hose for cleaning loose deposits and for flushing trash from sousaphones and tubas. This method will alleviate some problems, but it should not replace the methodical techniques previously mentioned.

Summer Cleaning

The lure of summer vacation affects the band director as much as it does his students, but the year's work is not complete until he is assured that all school brasses not going to the repair shop have been thoroughly cleaned *and dried* before storing. This should be done faithfully, whether the instruments are cleaned personally or by some other method.

Slide Greasing

After each washing, slides should be greased with cork grease or mutton tallow*. Where possible, the grease should be applied to each tube* separately, inserted into the sleeve* of the tube, and worked back and forth in a spiralling motion to coat the entire surface.

The tuning slides that are operated while playing, such as the first and third slides on cornets and trumpets, and the main tuning slide on some tubas, should be lubricated with a lighter solution. Castor oil or a mixture of castor oil and valve oil are liquids used by some professionals to assure maximum sealing and smooth operation.

Valve Oiling

A variety of opinions has been expressed concerning the need for and the frequency of valve oiling, but a repairman who has witnessed the destructive action of saliva acids and the wearing effect on pistons* from dry operation will attest to the necessity for oiling. One drop on each piston before playing will assure smooth operation and protect the finish against acids.

French horns that do not have hollow stems* for oiling should be oiled by placing several drops into the appropriate slide. Turn the instrument so that the oil will reach both ends of the rotary valve* and simultaneously operate the valve levers*. To make sure that oil reaches the critical points, the valve caps* should be removed and oil placed in the center of each bearing washer*. Since many rotary valve problems are caused by dry or corroded stems on the bearing washer side, the necessity for keeping these parts oiled is obvious.

PERCUSSIONS

Storing

Vital budget money can be saved each year if the director will devote a little attention to the proper storage of the percussion instruments. Valuable storage and protective devices can be easily devised with little expense. This will completely eliminate damage or loss. Figures 1, 2, and 3 illustrate only one of many solutions for storing mallets, sticks, and cymbals.

The brackets can be made from scrap material and mounted on a cabinet, a wall, or a door near the percussion section. A quick check by the percussion leader at the end of each band period will eliminate loss or misplacement.

In addition to the hinged, fibreboard protector ("General Precautions," page 3), padded covers (available at music stores), or muslin covers, made by a local upholstery firm, seat cover shop, or home economics department will offer protection against dust, fingerprints, and unauthorized tampering.

END
VIEW

TOP VIEW

FIGURE 1
Mallet holder

TOP VIEW

FIGURE 2
Snare drum stick holder

END VIEW

FIGURE 3
Cymbal holder
(Front view)

Setting Up

Many punctured snare heads and stretched snares are caused by care-less placement of the snare drums on the stand. A word of caution to the percussion players will often eliminate such accidents.

Hardware

Light petroleum grease or mutton tallow* should be used on the tension rod* threads. Household oil should be placed periodically on the moving parts of the snare strainer to assure smooth operation.

Shell

Mahogany shells should be cleaned and polished like fine furniture. A combination cleaner and wax, used occasionally, will help maintain a "new" look. A scratch remover polish will help cover the nicks and scratches that inevitably come with use.

Plastic shells may be cleaned with kerosene, cleaning wax, or any mild, non-abrasive cleaner.

Mallet Instruments

The polished metal areas (including the bars*) on glockenspiels, orchestra bells, chimes, xylophones, marimbas, and vibraphones should be wiped with a treated cloth after each handling.

Periodic dusting with a soft paint brush will prevent the build-up of dust in inaccessible places, particularly around the grommets* on glockenspiel bars.

The bearing areas on vibraphones should be oiled periodically, according to frequency of use, with a light household oil or whatever is recommended by the manufacturer. Broken drive belts and burned-out motors are the result of inadequate oiling procedures.

Drum Head Cleaning

Plastic drum heads should be cleaned with soap and water. Clean calfskin heads with an art gum eraser. A paint brush can be used to remove dust from around the hoops.

Accessories

Moving parts on the damper mechanism of chimes, tympani pedals, the hi-hat, bass drum, and the casters on movable percussions should be oiled periodically for longer life and proper operation.

SPECIFIC PRECAUTIONS

1. Do not lay a woodwind instrument on its keys.
2. Remove the bocal when carrying an assembled bassoon.

3. Always remove the sousaphone neckpipe* after playing.

4. Do not lay a sousaphone on its bell without removing the neckpipe.

5. Always *hold* a trombone when it is un-cased. Do not set it on a chair or lay it on the floor.

6. Always place a reed cap over the clarinet or saxophone mouthpiece when the instrument is not being played.

7. Avoid storing wood instruments in attics or basements.

ASSEMBLING THE WOODWINDS

Piccolo-Flute

1. Hold the head joint firmly.

2. Grip the main body near the tenon socket (Figures 4 and 5) so that no strain is placed on the hinge rods and tubings.

3. Insert the tenon with a twisting motion.

4. Hold the foot joint so that the fingers are arched over the hinge rod (Figure 6).

FIGURE 4
Assembling the piccolo

FIGURE 5
Inserting the flute head joint

5. While holding the flute body near the tenon socket, push the foot joint on with a slight twist.

FIGURE 6
Assembling the flute foot joint

Oboe-English Horn

In each step of assembling the oboe and English horn, grip the joints so that pressure exists only between the palm and the fingertips, with the fingers arched over the hinge rods. Push into position with a slight twisting motion. Carefully avoid damage to the bridge keys and spatulas*.

FIGURE 7
Step 1 Oboe

FIGURE 8
Step 1 English Horn

Close the low B♭ key with the thumb when assembling the oboe bell (Figure 9).

FIGURE 9
Step 2 Oboe

FIGURE 10
Step 2 English Horn

With the thumb and first finger on the top edge of the cork, push and twist the reed and bocal into position (Figures 11 and 12).

FIGURE 11
Step 3 Oboe

FIGURE 12
Step 3 English Horn

FIGURE 13
Step 4 English Horn

Bassoon

1. Set the boot joint on a chair, table, or on the floor.

2. With the right hand, hold the boot joint so that no pressure is exerted on the hinge rods.

3. Insert the tenor and bass joints together (Figure 14), part way into the sockets. (Bassoons equipped with locking devices should be locked during this step.)

4. Unlock the tenor and bass joints.

5. With the first finger (left hand) hooked over the bocal socket*, *push* the tenor joint into position.

6. While holding the bass joint by the upper tenon, *push* the bass joint into position. Use caution to avoid key damage.

7. Hold the low B♭ key with the thumb (Figure 15) and *push* the bell onto the bass joint.

8. Hold the bocal as shown in Figure 16. Push and twist it into alignment with the whisper key.

FIGURE 14
Step 1 Bassoon

FIGURE 15
Step 2 Bassoon

FIGURE 16
Step 3 Bassoon

Soprano Clarinets

1. Upper and lower joints
   a) Grip the upper joint with the fingers pressing the ring keys.
   b) Hold the lower joint so that needed pressure is applied only to the body and the large pad cups.
   c) Connect the joints with a twisting motion.

2. Bell
   a) Hold the bottom joint with the fingers arched over the ring-key hinge rod.
   b) Place the bell on the tenon with a series of twists.

3. Barrel joint
   a) Hold the upper joint with body and ring key pressure.
   b) Place the barrel joint on the tenon with a twist.

4. Mouthpiece
   Hold the upper joint as in 3-a above. Insert the mouthpiece with a twist.

FIGURE 17
Step 1 Soprano clarinet

FIGURE 18
Step 2 Soprano clarinet

FIGURE 19
Step 3 Soprano clarinet

FIGURE 20
Step 4 Soprano clarinet

5. Reed
   Install as shown in Figure 21.

FIGURE 21
Step 5 Soprano clarinet

Alto and Bass Clarinets

1. Upper and lower joints
   a) Hold the upper joint with the fingers on the plateau keys.
   b) Grip the lower joint below the spatulas with the hand arched over the hinge rods.
   c) Connect the tenons with a slight twist, using caution to prevent bridge key damage.

2. Bell
   a) Hold the bell bow* in the palm with the fingers holding the low Eb pad closed.
   b) Place the bell on the tenon with a twist, and align the bridge keys.

FIGURE 22
Step 1 Large clarinet

FIGURE 23
Step 2 Large clarinet

3. Neckpipe
   a) Grip the neckpipe by the bow nearest the tenon.
   b) Insert the tenon in the upper joint socket, and align the octave bridge.

4. Mouthpiece
   a) Hold the neckpipe near the socket with the heel of the hand braced against the upper joint.
   b) Insert the mouthpiece.

FIGURE 24
Step 3 Large clarinet

FIGURE 25
Step 4 Large clarinet

Don Da Grade

2

Inspections

The following procedures may seem intricate and time consuming, yet one inspection will convince the director or instrumentalist of the importance of maintaining thorough, periodic inspections.

To *properly* test for instrument leakage, it is necessary for the director to place his mouth on many instruments to create a vacuum. It is advisable, therefore, to begin the inspection with clean cloths and an antiseptic solution for sterilization. On *unlacquered* instruments (oboe, clarinet, flutes), alcohol is quite effective. For other equipment, see the "Standard Repairs" chapter.

Although instrument malfunctions have a variety of causes, the testing procedures listed in this chapter should pinpoint the source of a majority of the problems and guide the director to the proper solution.

After each instrument is inspected visually and physically (as in the following procedures), it should be checked by playing with all fingering combinations.

PICCOLO-FLUTE

Visual Inspection

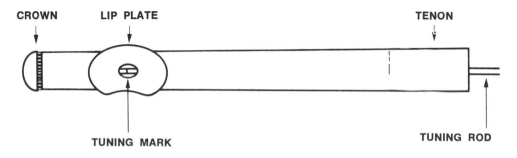

FIGURE 26
Flute tuning

1. Check the tuning cork* for proper setting, (Figure 26).

2. Check for a loose or missing crown.

3. Check for severe dents on all joints.

4. Check for accumulated dust or oil around keys and posts*.

5. Check the blow hole* for cleanliness.

6. Check the bore for dirt accumulation.

7. Check all pads to see if skins are moth eaten or frayed.

8. Check for missing pad screws* or washers*.

9. Check for bent keys.

10. Check to see if all keys open the same distance from the tone holes*.

11. Check the case hardware (hinges and latch) for security.

12. Check for the presence of a tuning rod and swab.

13. Check the case interior for cleanliness.

14. Check for loose pivot screws* and hinge rods*.

Physical Inspection

1. Check the head and foot joint tenons* for snug fits.

2. Check all keys for proper functioning:
   a) Does the thumb B♭ key close the thumb pad and the B♭ key simultaneously?
   b) Does the forked B♭ (first finger, right hand) key close the F, F♯,, and B♭ keys simultaneously?
   c) Do the D and E keys close simultaneously with the F♯?
   d) Does the low C lever* close the C♯ and C pads simultaneously?
   e) Is there a slack motion in any bridge key before it actuates its relative key?
   f) Is there a metallic sound when the keys are operated?
   g) Do all keys operate freely?
   h) Do the pads stick?

3. Check for loose action of hinge rods and hinge tubings*.

4. Check the head joint for leaks.
   a) After cleaning the lip plate and blow hole, place the palm of the left hand over the open tenon.
   b) Place the lips over the lip plate* and create a vacuum by sucking until portions of the lips are pulled into the blow hole. If the vacuum holds for at least fifteen seconds without releasing any pressure, there are no serious leaks.

Leaks are present if there is a release of pressure during the fifteen seconds.

c) To determine whether the leaks are in the tuning cork or in the solder around the lip plate, remove the crown and push the tuning cork* out of the *opposite end* (see Figure 57, page 72) with the tuning rod.

d) Cover the ends (which are now open) with both palms and again create a vacuum as in the preceding manner. If no leaks are present, the tuning cork is the source of the leak. If a leak is still present, the leak is around the soldered portion of the lip plate. Only an experienced repairman should re-solder the lip plate.

5. Check the body for leaks.
   a) Place a cork stopper in the foot tenon.
   b) Lightly cover the keys as in fingering low D.
   c) Place the lips on the head joint socket* and create a vacuum.
   d) If the vacuum does not hold, a leak is present. The seriousness of the leak can be determined by the speed of a vacuum release. Inability to create a vacuum is an indication of one or more serious leaks. Follow the repair procedures listed in the "Standard Repairs" chapter.
   e) Blow lightly into the body part to check for weak springs.

6. Check the foot joint* for leaks.
   a) Hold the palm of one hand over the bottom end.
   b) Lightly close the low C key.
   c) Create a vacuum with the mouth on the tenon end.
   d) Follow the same procedures as in Number 5, d) and e) above.

   Note: Though leaks should be located visually, or with the aid of a feeler* when possible, blowing smoke through the stopped instrument will quickly reveal leaks which may be difficult to locate. When working alone, a mirror is helpful for locating leaks in pads which are not in the visual range.

OBOE-ENGLISH HORN

Visual Inspection

1. Check the reed for chips, cracks, opening and strength.
2. Check all tenons for chipped areas and frayed tenon corks.

3. Check all body parts for cracks.

4. Check for dust and oil around keys and posts*.

5. Check for worn or frayed skin pads.

6. Check the bore of all body parts for cleanliness.

7. Check the automatic octave keys for proper operation.

8. Check all keys for proper opening from tone holes.

9. Check for bent or broken keys.

10. Check the case hardware for security.

11. Check for cleaning swabs, cork grease, and tenon caps.

12. Check the case interior for cleanliness.

13. Check the tone holes.
    a) Are they dirty?
    b) Are they chipped?

14. Check the English horn bocals.
    a) Do they need new cork?
    b) Are they dirty or damaged?

15. Check for loose pivot screws and hinge rods.

Physical Inspection

1. Check all keys for proper functioning:
    a) Do all bridge keys close their related pads?
    b) Do the keys respond quickly or are they sluggish?
    c) Is the inaction of a key caused by a broken or unhooked needle spring*?
    d) Is there unnecessary noise caused by missing key corks?
    e) Is the sluggish action of a key caused by a loose or twisted post?

2. Check for loose tenon rings.

3. Check for leaks in the upper joint.
    a) Place a stopper in the tenon end.
    b) Place the fingers over the keys as though fingering G.
    c) Place the mouth over the reed socket* and create a vacuum.
    d) Follow the previously mentioned techniques (Flute, Physical Inspection, pages 28 and 29) for determining the presence and location of leaks.

4. Check for leaks in the lower joint.
    a) Place a stopper in the *middle* tenon socket.

    b) Using both hands, lightly close the keys as though fingering low Bb.

    c) Place the mouth over (or in) the bell tenon and create a vacuum.

    d) Follow the standard leak-finding procedures.

5. Check the tenons for snug fits.

6. Check the thumb rest for cork and tightness.

CLARINETS

Visual Inspection

1. Check the mouthpiece.
   a) Are there nicked or chipped areas on the rails or the tip?
   b) Is it clean?
   c) Does the ligature fit properly?
   d) Is the reed chipped, cracked, or extremely weak?
   e) Is the cork satisfactory?

2. Check the body parts for cracks.

3. Check all tenons for frayed corks and chipped areas.

4. Check the tone holes.
   a) Are they chipped?
   b) Are they dirty?

5. Check the bores for evidence of improper swabbing.

6. Check for loose pivot screws and hinge rods.

7. Check for cleanliness around posts and keys.

8. Check for broken or bent keys.

9. Check for frayed or moth-eaten pads.

10. Check all keys for proper opening.

11. Check the alto and bass clarinet bell.
    a) Does the low Eb (bell key) close simultaneously with low E and F?
    b) Are there serious dents in the bell bow?
    c) Is the bell bow brace unsoldered?
    d) Is the low Eb key corked to prevent bridge key noises?

12. Check the case hinges and latches for proper security.

13. Check the case for swabs, cork grease, and mouthpiece cap.

14. Check the case for cleanliness.

Physical Inspection

1. Check all bridge keys for proper operation.
   a) Is there loose action between A and A♭ (G♯)?
   b) Does the forked E♭-B♭ fingering close the upper joint pad properly?
   c) Is there loose play between the low G♯ (A♭) presser foot* and the low E and F♯ spatula*?
   d) Can the clarinet slur from a fourth line D to the third line B without squeaking?

2. Check all joints for snug fits.

3. Check all keys for fast response.

4. Check the tenon and bell rings for tightness.

5. Check the upper joint for leaks.
   a) Place the palm of the right hand over the middle tenon.
   b) Finger middle C.
   c) Place the lips in the upper tenon and create a vacuum.
   d) Follow the procedure mentioned previously for locating leaks (Flute, Physical Inspection, pages 28 and 29.)

6. Check the lower joint for leaks.
   a) Place the palm of the left hand over the bell tenon.
   b) Finger low E.
   c) Place the mouth on the middle tenon socket and create a vacuum.
   d) Follow the normal leak finding procedure.

7. Check the bass and contrabass clarinets for leaks. Using a leak light,* check the upper joint as follows:
   a) Check the closed keys (A, A♭, and C♯).
   b) Depress the thumb key and check it and its relative key (opposite side of the body) for simultaneous closings.
   c) Check each finger key and its relative key as in b) above.
   d) If the octave or register key(s) are too small to emit light, they should be checked for proper closing with a feeler.
   e) Follow the procedures in the "Standard Repairs" chapter for re-seating or replacing leaking pads.

8. Check the lower joint on the bass and contrabass clarinets with a leak light as follows:
   a) Check the closed pads (F♯-B trill, low F♯ and low G♯).
   b) Check the main line or stack* pads.
   c) Check the bridge keys for simultaneous closings.
   d) Follow the standard repair procedures to eliminate leaks.

9. Check all keys for proper corking.
10. Check all pads for looseness.

   Note: Using a pencil-shaped typewriter eraser (with a pointed end), lightly touch each pad on front and back sides to see if the pad will fall out. This procedure will often eliminate the annoying loose pad problems that seemingly occur prior to every concert!

BASSOONS

Visual Inspection

1. Check the reeds for splitting or chipping.
2. Check the bocals*.
   a) Are they properly corked?
   b) Are they dirty?
   c) Are they bent or damaged?
   d) Are the nibs* stopped up? (To prevent nib damage, use only a thin, non-metallic straw or bristle when cleaning the hole.)
3. Check for bent or broken keys.
4. Check the joint lock for security.
   a) Are its screws loose?
   b) Is it bent or broken?
5. Check the crutch and crutch holder for looseness.
6. Check for loose pivot screws or hinge rods.
7. Check for frayed or loose pads.
8. Check the tone holes for dents or chipped areas.
9. Check all bores for improper swabbing.
10. Check the end bow* for evidences of leaks around the flange*. (The bow cap* can usually be removed easily with a slight pressure.)
11. Check for dirt and excessive oil around the posts and keys.
12. Check all tenons.
   a) Are the corks worn or loose?
   b) Are there chipped areas?
13. Check the case hardware for security.
14. Check the case for the presence of cork grease, swabs, and strap.
15. Check the case for cleanliness.

Physical Inspection

1. Check all keys for proper functioning.
   a) Do all bridge mechanisms operate in unison?
   b) Do the keys respond freely?
   c) Are there unnecessary noises?
   d) Is there slack in bridge keys before response?
   e) Are there broken or unhooked springs?
   f) Do the keys open the proper distance from tone holes?
   g) Does the whisper key function properly?

2. Check all tenons for snug fit.

3. Check for loose pads. (Follow the procedure as described for clarinets.)

4. Check the tenon rings or bands for looseness.

5. Check the tenor joint for leaks.
   a) Place a stopper in the bocal socket.
   b) Using both hands, close all keys.
   c) Place the mouth in the tenon and create a vacuum.
   d) For finding leaks in the bassoon, the leak light and feeler must be used jointly. This is due to the shape of some tone holes, keys guards, and the varying size of the bore.

6. Check the butt* or boot* joint for leaks.
   a) Place a stopper in one of the tenon sockets.
   b) Close the keys.
   c) Place the mouth in the other tenon socket and create a vacuum.
   d) Follow the standard leak finding procedures.

7. Check the bass joint for leaks. Follow procedure as in Number 5 and Number 6 above.

   Note: Due to the nature of the wood, the texture of the pad skins and the size of the bassoon, it is difficult to form a tight vacuum.

8. Check the bell joint for leaks (leak light testing).

SAXOPHONES

Visual Inspection

1. Check the mouthpiece.
   a) Is it clean?

b) Is it cracked on the tenon end? (An indication of improper corking.)

c) Are the rails and the tip dented or chipped?

d) Does the ligature fit properly?

e) Is the reed in good condition?

2. Check the neckpipe.
   a) Is it corked properly?
   b) Is it dirty inside?
   c) Is the octave pad skin eaten away by saliva acids?
   d) Is the tenon warped or dented?
   e) Is the hinge rod loose?

3. Check the body.
   a) Are there serious dents?
   b) Is there evidence of poor swabbing? Green stains inside the bell bow* and dark, dried, or brittle low D♯ (E♭) pad indicate improper drying.

4. Check for bent or broken keys.

5. Check for proper key opening.

6. Check for dark or frayed pads.

7. Check the case hardware for security.

8. Check the case for swabs, mouthpiece cap, end plug, and a sturdy accessory compartment.

9. Check the case for cleanliness.

10. Check for loose pivot screws and hinge rods.

11. Check for loose bell-to-body brace.

12. Check for loose or missing key guards.

Physical Inspection

1. Check all keys.
   a) Do all keys respond freely?
   b) Do the bridge keys operate in unison?
   c) Is there slack motion in the bridge keys?
   d) Do the key rollers on the table keys operate freely?

2. Check for loose pads. Use an eraser as in clarinet pad testing.

3. Check all pads for leaks.
   a) Using a leak light, check all closed pads starting with the upper (palm*) F.
   b) Check the upper stack pads and their relative bridge keys for simultaneous closings.

    c) Check the lower stack and low C pads.

    d) Check the bridge mechanisms as in b) above. In particular, finger F while fingering G♯, and check both pads for leaks.

    e) Check the bell keys and their proper bridge functionings.

    Note: To test for leaks in the baritone or bass saxophone, the side B♭ key must be removed and the leak light inserted through the B♭ tone hole. The low C or the low D♯ key must then be removed for checking the side B♭ pad.

4. Check the octave mechanism.
   a) Finger G above the staff.
   b) Is the low octave key open and the neck octave key closed?
   c) Finger A above the staff.
   d) Does the neck octave open and the low octave close?

PISTON VALVE INSTRUMENTS

Visual Inspection

1. Check the mouthpiece.
   a) Does it need re-plating?
   b) Is the shank bent or oval shaped?
   c) Is the throat* clean and free from obstruction?
   d) Are there dents in the rim?

2. Check for serious dents.

3. Check for loose braces.

4. Check the valve ports* and tuning slide interiors for evidence of improper cleaning.

5. Check for missing fingerbuttons*, pull knobs*, bottom valve caps*, fingerhooks*, lyre holders, lyre screws, and water keys*.

6. Check for mis-shaped thumb rings*, finger rings*, and fingerhooks.

7. Check the case hardware for security.

8. Check the case interior for a sturdy accessory compartment and cleanliness.

9. Check the case compartment for valve oil, slide grease, lyre, and a chamois skin.

10. Check the sousaphone neckpipe*, gooseneck*, and tuning bits* for damage.

11. Check the sousaphone and other adjustable bell brasses for loose or missing bell spuds* and bell screws*.

12. Check the pistons*.
    a) Broad worn spots indicate oval shaped casings.
    b) A thin worn line indicates a dent in the casing.
    c) Flaking or peeling of the piston* finish indicates poor plating.
    d) A tarnished piston indicates use of saliva as a lubricant.

13. Check the finger buttons for even alignment.

14. Check the piston alignment by determining whether the indented ring marks on the piston stems* are level with the tops of the upper valve caps. (Figure 76, page 101.)

15. Check the water key corks.

Physical Inspection

1. Check all slides for ease of removal.

2. Check the valves for spring tension and fast response.

3. Check the top and bottom valve caps for easy removal.

4. Check suspected leaks by stopping one end of the tube and forcing air pressure into the other end.

5. Check water key springs for proper tension.

ROTARY VALVE INSTRUMENTS

Visual Inspection

1. Check the mouthpiece as in the Piston Valve Instruments section.

2. Check for severe dents.

3. Check for loose braces.

4. Check the slide interiors for improper cleaning.

5. Check the alignment of each valve port.
    a) Remove the bottom valve cap.
    b) Locate the alignment mark at the end of the rotor shaft (Figure 27).
    c) Depress and release the valve key to determine if the marks on the shaft align with the mark on the bearing washer*.

FIGURE 27
Aligning the rotary valve

6. Check for alignment of keys.

7. Check the case hardware for security.

8. Check the case interior.
   a) Is there a sturdy strap?
   b) Are there loose articles?
   c) Is it clean?

9. Check the valve strings for wear and for proper size and type.

10. Check for missing fingerhook, pull rings*, lyre holders, and lyre screws.

Physical Inspection

1. Check all slides for ease of removal.

2. Check all valves for correct spring tension and quick response.

3. Check the valve action for slack in the strings.

4. Check the valve action for unnecessary noise.

TROMBONE

Visual Inspection

1. Check the mouthpiece as in the Piston Valve Instruments section.

2. Check for proper cleanliness.
    a) Remove the inner slides and sight through each bore.
    b) Pull the tuning slide and inspect the tubing interior.

3. Check the water key cork.

4. Check for bad dents in the bell, bell tubing, tuning slide, and hand slide bow*.

5. Check the case hardware for security.

6. Check the case interior.
    a) Are the turnbuttons or straps in good condition?
    b) Is the accessory compartment in good condition?
    c) Is the case clean?
    d) Are the lyre and cleaning rod holding mechanisms adequate to prevent them from coming loose in the case?

7. Check the stockings* for signs of improper cleaning procedures (accumulation of deposits), and for improper slide alignment (worn spots).

Physical Inspection

1. Check the tuning slide for easy removal.

2. Check the hand slide for smooth action.
    a) Before assembling, place the slides vertically with the slide bow resting on the floor.
    b) Slowly lift the inner slides to check for dents or rough spots.
    c) Place the slides in playing position. Release the hand slide and see if gravity will move it to the sixth or seventh position.

3. Check the hand slide for compression.
    a) Hold the slide vertically with the open ends down.
    b) Lift the hand slide up to sixth or seventh position.
    c) Stop both openings of the inner tubings.
    d) Release the hand slide. A tight slide will require several seconds for gravity to bring it to first position. A loose and leaking slide will descend much more rapidly. Loss of compression is sometimes caused by a poor water key cork or a weak water key spring. This can be further checked by removing the inner slide, closing one end of the hand slide and blowing into the other end.

4. Check for adequate slide bumper corks by lightly bumping the hand slide to first position.

5. Check the slide lock for a secure fit.

DRUMS

Visual Inspection

1. Check the batter and snare heads for holes, breaks, and for cleanliness.
2. Check the shell and metallic parts for evidences of improper care (dents, scratches, rust, and dirt).
3. Check the hoops for even or level installation.
4. Check the snares for correct size and placement on the head.
5. Check for dust accumulation around the hoop.
6. Check for missing tension rods and broken strainer parts.
7. Check for proper greasing of tension rods.
8. Check for stretched or broken snare strands.
9. Check for frayed or broken snare attachment cords.

Physical Inspection

1. Check the snare strainer for smooth operation.
2. Check the snare strainer for correct pressure and release.
3. Check the head tension at each tension rod.

TIMPANI

Visual Inspection

1. Check for severe dents in the shell.
2. Check for missing or broken tension rods.
3. Check the head for cleanliness.
4. Check the head for breaks.
5. Check the head for a proper collar and even (level) application of tension by all rods.
6. Check the tension rods for greasing.

Physical Inspection

1. Check the pedal for proper tension, release, and holding.

2. Check for unnecessary noises when the pedal is operated.

3. Check the casters for proper operation.

MALLET INSTRUMENTS

Visual Inspection

1. Check each instrument for dust accumulation and filmy deposits on bars* and tubes.

2. Check for loose bars caused by worn grommets* or a broken bar-retaining cord.

3. Check for broken, bent, or disconnected damper mechanisms.

4. Check the resonating tubes for dents and cracks.

Physical Inspection

1. Check the pulsators (on vibes) for free action. (Bent pulsator rods, improper oiling, and dirt accumulation will often cause irregular pulsations.)

2. Check the resonator speed controls, drive belts, and pulleys for proper functioning. A frayed or stretched belt, a loose pulley, or a burned-out rheostat can also cause irregular pulsations.

3. Check the casters for free, rolling actions. Accumulations of lint, dust, loose strands from floor mops, etc., often become wound around the axle of the casters.

4. Check each bar individually for correct musical response. (Worn grommets on bell lyras can cause a metallic rattle. Slack in the bar retaining cord can muffle the marimba notes.)

CYMBALS AND GONGS

Visual and Physical Inspection

1. Check for cracks (see the "Standard Repairs" chapter for repairs).

2. Check the cymbal holders and gong support cord.
   a) Are they worn or frayed?
   b) Do they prevent a clear response?

3. Check the gong stand for rigidity.

4. Check for proper storage and handling.

PERCUSSION ACCESSORIES

Visual and Physical Inspection

1. Check all small accessories (wood blocks, tambourines, etc.) for broken parts.

2. Check the snare and bass drum stands.
   a) Is it good, sturdy equipment that is not likely to collapse?
   b) Are the threads stripped on the tightening screws?
   c) Are the rubber crutch tips deteriorated?
   d) Are the sleeves (for snare drum stand-arms) in good condition?
   e) Does the cradle felt for the bass drum stand need replacing?

3. Check the bass drum pedal (stage band) for proper care.
   a) Is the strap worn or broken?
   b) Has it been oiled properly?
   c) Do all tension screws work properly?
   d) Is the action free?
   e) Has the beater been rotated to prevent wear on one side?
   f) Has oil and dust accumulated around the working parts?

4. Check all mallets and beaters for loose heads.

5. Check all snare drum sticks for jagged or broken tips.

3

Suggested Repair Equipment

The equipment listed in this chapter has been organized into separate sections in order of priority, to accommodate each instrumentalist's skill, his budget, and his nearness to a competent repairman.

Many items in List A should be standard equipment in *every* school that has a band program, even though repair service may be ideal. It is doubtful that any administrator would be reluctant to spend the small amount necessary to purchase repair equipment that could mean eventual savings which far exceed the initial cost. Few directors wish to lose valuable student hours due to the lack of basic items of repair equipment needed for emergencies.

Each succeeding section (B, C, etc.) presupposes that the director has purchased the tools and equipment given in previous sections, and that he is qualified to proceed with more difficult repairs.

To determine the current price for each item and to become familiar with the tools and equipment, the director should consult one or more of the repair supply catalogs listed in the bibliography.

Most instrumentalists, with a little manual skill, can make many of the tools, but the time required to make them does not justify the effort. The only exception is, possibly, the feelers* which can be made of wooden matches and a thin strip of cellophane (i.e. a cigarette band).

LIST A. FIRST PRIORITY TOOLS AND SUPPLIES

Tools

1. One mouthpiece puller (preferably with various sized collars)
2. One clarinet screw driver, preferably with swivel top, a six inch blade, and a short reversible blade
3. One saxophone screw driver

4. One pad slick

5. One bunsen burner (An alcohol burner is not as satisfactory.)

6. One pair of six inch, flat nose pliers (smooth jaws)

7. A one inch rawhide mallet

8. A *good* four inch vise

9. Three feelers*

10. One cornet-trumpet mandrel for holding instruments in the vise while polishing, removing stuck slides, etc.

11. A flexible trombone cleaning brush, which can be used for *all* brass instruments

12. One mouthpiece brush (woodwinds)

13. One mouthpiece brush (brasses)

14. A set of testing corks

15. One spring hook

16. One clarinet assembly board

17. One pin vise

Supplies

1. One can of penetrating oil

2. A tube of liquid shellac

3. One hundred assorted, tapered water key corks

4. One hundred assorted felt washers

5. One hundred assorted cork washers

6. One dozen 3/16″ x 1½″ French horn corks

7. One hundred assorted, double skin and beveled, medium thickness clarinet pads. These can also be used for piccolo, oboe, and flute (small pads only) in an emergency.

8. One jar of mutton tallow (See Mutton Tallow in the "Terminology" chapter.)

9. One hundred assorted saxophone (felt) key bumpers

10. One hundred assorted saxophone key-felts

11. One hundred silencer skins (for left hand levers on clarinets)

12. One spool of French horn valve cord (twenty pound linen line)

13. Six feet of cord for attaching snares onto drums

14. One can of non-abrasive brass polish

15. An assortment of rags

16. Two single-edged razor blades

17. One package of paper for cleaning eyeglasses

18. One bottle of alcohol or a good disinfectant

19. One package of pipe cleaners

20. Six sticks of white pad cement

21. One dozen thumb-rest screws

22. One bottle of key oil

LIST B. SELECT FROM THIS LIST AFTER THE PURCHASE OF LIST A TOOLS AND SUPPLIES

Tools

1. Leak light

2. One set of wedges for removing stuck trombone tapers

3. One valve mirror

4. One bench knife

5. One pair of round nose pliers (six inches)

6. One set of key leveling wedges for saxophones

7. One saxophone assembly board

8. One set of tone hole reamers for removing chipped tone holes on clarinets

9. One hooked scraper for removing old joint cork

10. One straight scraper for cleaning shellac from grooves in tenons

11. One valve cleaning rod

12. One emory stone

13. One shellac spatula

Supplies

1. One hundred assorted saxophone pads

2. Four sheets of fine garnet paper

3. Four shellac sticks

4. One sheet of ⅛ inch cork

5. One assortment of key cork

6. One bottle of contact cement

7. A small bottle of powdered pumice

8. Two sheets of extra fine waterproof abrasive paper

LIST C. TO BE PURCHASED ONLY AFTER THE SKILLS REQUIRED FOR LISTS A AND B HAVE BEEN DEVELOPED

Tools

1. One jeweler's anvil

2. One tenon* expander (can opener type)

3. One set of saxophone key bending tools

4. One ½ inch (.5000) trombone slide mandrel (for removing dents in trombone slides)

5. One flute key opening gauge

6. One dent hammer (small)

7. One cork protector (for re-corking saxophone necks)

8. One assembly board for flutes

9. One needle spring pliers (for removing whole needle springs)

10. One vernier caliper

11. One flute head joint expander

12. One six inch mill file

13. One pair of common slip-joint pliers

Supplies

1. Six flute head corks*

2. One dozen straight saxophone neck corks (eight for the alto, four for the tenor and baritone)

3. One dozen post shims

4. One hundred assorted flat springs (clarinet)

5. One hundred assorted flat springs (saxophones)

6. One dozen flat spring screws

7. Three feet of heavy cotton cord

8. One foot of .025 flute spring wire

9. Six piccolo head corks

LIST D. ADEQUATE TIME MUST BE ALLOWED FOR THE USE OF ITEMS IN THIS LIST

Tools

1. One pair of six inch diagonal cutters
2. One pair of needle spring* pliers for removing broken needle springs
3. One tone hole* file
4. One awl
5. One jeweler's saw frame
6. One dozen jeweler's saw blades
7. One oboe assembly board
8. Twelve flute pad-clamps

Supplies

1. An assortment of clarinet and saxophone pivot screws*. Since sizes vary according to instrument type and brand, the director will be wise to order only a dozen for each of the brands that are popular in his area.
2. One hundred assorted needle springs
3. Four dozen assorted water key springs (one dozen each of the four most popular sizes)
4. One hundred assorted double skin flute pads
5. One hundred thin, flute pad washers (twenty-five of each size—16, 17, 18, and 19 mm)

LIST E. THIS LIST SHOULD BE CONSIDERED ONLY BY INSTRUMENTALISTS TO WHOM REPAIR FACILITIES ARE NOT ACCESSIBLE, OR WHO HAVE UNUSUAL MECHANICAL ABILITY

Tools

1. One set pivot screw reamers
2. One set pivot screw counter-sinking reamers

3. One set hinge tube shorteners

4. One head mandrel (flute)

5. One body mandrel (flute)

6. One ½″ x 1″ x 30″ tapered mandrel (for removing dents in cornet, trumpet, and trombone bell tubing)

7. One bassoon assembly board

8. One 21/32″ to 23/32″ expandable reamer (for removing dents from cornet casings)

9. One trombone bumper cork remover

10. One set of number drills, 1 through 60

11. One hand or electric drill

Supplies

1. One hundred assorted oboe pads

2. One hundred assorted pads for alto and bass clarinets and bassoon

3. One fifteen-inch piece of roller* tubing for saxophone keys

4. One set of ebony compound and solvent

5. One sheet of 3/32″ x 4″ x 12″ cork

Persons who desire to learn more about soldering, drilling, polishing, burnishing, major dent work, crack pinning, swedging, and lathe work should consult their local repairman for assistance. Such techniques cannot be described easily, and the equipment is quite expensive.

Standard Repairs

Inexperienced instrumentalists are prone to make mistakes in their first repair attempts. This is due, primarily, to the variety of structural weaknesses in each instrument, its age, its brand, its type, the care it has received, etc. It is doubtful, however, whether anyone who follows safe repair practices could cause irreparable damage to any instrument. It is probable that he will receive genuine satisfaction from a successful repair attempt.

The problems in this chapter are the ones most frequently encountered by the average director. While some will have difficulties with the simplest repairs, others will be able to follow the most difficult procedures. Each director, therefore, must judge for himself what repairs he should attempt. The following points should be considered before making this decision:

1. The actual need (distance to a reliable repairman, band budget, etc.)
2. Time
3. Personal interest
4. Dexterity (This can be developed if the interest is strong.)
5. Availability of old instruments on which to practice

After each heading (A, B, etc.), in the following chapter, the tools and/or supplies are listed which will be necessary for the given repair. It should be mentioned again that the tools and supplies have been given in order of required proficiency, and this order should be ignored only at the director's risk. For instance, use of the tenon expanders might necessitate the filing away of precious metal around a flute head or foot joint, or a saxophone neck tenon, if the director has not first discovered the malleability of brass as evidenced in pulling stuck slides or bending saxophone keys for re-leveling pad cups. Therefore, if the director has only the tools and experience required in the A and B lists, a repair problem that requires tools from Lists D or E usually should be left to a professional repairman.

GENERAL WOODWIND PROCEDURES

Preparing Key Cork
(List B Supplies)

1. Select several thicknesses of cork and apply a thin coat of contact cement on one side of each piece.

2. Allow them to dry thoroughly (one hour) and place them in a dust free container that will not allow the coated sides to touch.

3. When needed, the cemented side will adhere readily to a clean, heated key.

Corking Keys
(List B Tools and Supplies)

1. Scrape off the old cork.

2. Heat the area to be corked just beyond the point where it is comfortable to the touch (overheating will burn the lacquer on saxophone keys).

3. Apply the coated side of the cork (Figure 28) to the underside of the key.

4. Press the corked area against the key until cool.

5. With a razor blade or a knife, trim so that all sides are beveled. (Figure 29)

FIGURE 28
Corking the key
(Top view)

FIGURE 29
Trimmed cork
(Side and end views)

FIGURE 30
Removing excess key cork

6. If the cork is too thick, slip a strip of fine garnet paper (with the rough side towards cork) under the key, depress the key lightly and pull garnet paper out (Figure 30). Repeat until desired thickness is obtained.

Preparing Garnet Paper

1. Cut into ½ inch or ⅝ inch wide strips which can be used for sanding tenons (Figure 42, page 58), or in removing key cork (as in Number 6 above).

2. Another helpful use of garnet paper is to glue strips of it to both sides of a thin (⅛ x ½ x 8 inch) slat for smoothing key cork edges. If used this way, several slats should be made at one time and kept available for immediate use.

Installing Glued Pads
(List B Tools and Supplies)

The following process includes the C key and trill keys on flutes, all pads on clarinets, oboes, bassoons, and most saxophones. Piccolo pads require special treatment.

1. Remove the key from the instrument.

2. Remove the old pad and the glue with a screw driver.

3. Select the correct pad size.

4. Puncture the pad (Figure 31) with a needle or pin (white skin pads only) to let the heated air escape.

5. Hold the key over the flame for two or three seconds (longer for larger keys).

6. Apply the white glue stick to the inside of the cup and let enough melt to cover the bottom. A shellac stick is preferable for gluing kid skin pads.

   Note: The white glue and shellac sticks may be heated and tapered to a point for easier application in the smaller cups.

7. While the glue is still in liquid form, press the pad in the cup. The saxophone pad should be pressed firmly into the cup by holding it level against a clean, flat surface while cooling.

8. Install the key on the instrument.

PUNCTURE HERE

FIGURE 31
Puncturing the pad

Seating Glued Pads (except for saxophones)
(List A Tools and Supplies)

1. With a feeler or leak light*, locate the points of strong and weak contact of the pad against the tone hole (Figure 32).

FIGURE 32
Testing the pad seating

FIGURE 33
Heating the mounted key

2. Heat the pad as in Figure 33, using caution to prevent burning the pad or the instrument.

3. Shift the pad with a pad slick (Figure 34) until it contacts the tone hole evenly on all sides. It may be necessary to repeat these three steps several times before a satisfactory covering* is obtained.

FIGURE 34
Shifting the pad

Seating Glued Pads (Saxophones)
(List C Tools and Supplies)

Although several keys on the saxophone can be seated* with key leveling wedges and finger pressure (or light taps of the rawhide mallet), others such as the stack* and bell keys should be leveled with the key bending tools as listed in "C" tools. Body dents, bent hinge rods*, and loose tone holes* (soldered type) are often results of careless leveling attempts with the rawhide mallet.

1. Using the leak light*, locate the strong and weak contact points of the pad.

2. Place a leveling wedge under the strong contact point (the area of the pad that touches the tone hole first).

3. Apply pressure on the weak side (Figure 35).

4. Repeat the first three steps as often as necessary to seat the pad satisfactorily.

5. For a smoother coverage after seating, wet the pad thoroughly and place a cork wedge under the key foot (to hold the pad against the tone hole), and allow several hours for drying.

6. Remove the cork wedge and test for leakage.

FIGURE 35
Leveling the saxophone key

Installing and Seating Flute Pads
(List D Tools and Supplies)

The following procedures are for large pads on the average, student model flutes. Due to the intricacy of the French open hole models, the director should not attempt to replace leaking pads on them nor to do more than make the necessary, minor adjustments.

1. Remove the key(s) from the flute. (See page 55, Flute Repad, No. 1.)

2. Unscrew the pad screw(s)*.

3. With a needle or small screw driver, remove the old pad(s) and paper washer(s) (shims*).

4. Insert a new pad, but do not insert the paper shims.

5. Attach the metal washer and the pad screw.

6. Install the key on the flute.

7. Using the feeler*, test for strong and weak contact points.

8. The pad should exert slightly more pressure on the back side (hinge rod* side) than on the front (outside).

9. If the back side of the pad touches only slightly or not at all, repeat the above procedures. Each time add paper washers under the pad until the desired pressure is obtained.

10. Wet the pad with a pad slick and remove wrinkles from the skin.

FIGURE 36
Applying the pad clamp.

11. Place pad clamp(s) over the key(s) (Figure 36) and allow to dry for several hours, preferably overnight.

12. Remove clamp(s) and test the pad with a feeler.

13. If extra shims should be necessary after drying, mark the pad's location in the cup (Figure 37), add shim(s), and replace the pad in its original position.

FIGURE 37
Marking the pad's position

14. Repeat any of the previous steps that are necessary in obtaining a smooth, well-seated pad.

Flute Repad
(List D Tools and Supplies)

Although a *good,* complete flute repad* demands much time and skill, the following procedure is given for the director who wishes to pursue repairs to this point.

1. Remove all keys in the following order and place the screws in the mounting board.

   a) Thumb key
   b) Upper C hinge rod*
   c) D pivot screw*
   d) Remove all main line keys.
   e) Remove the G hinge rod and key (two pad cups).
   f) Remove the trill key pivot screws and keys.
   g) Remove G♯ hinge rod and key.
   h) Remove the foot joint hinge rod and keys.

2. Remove the old pads and replace with new ones as described in the previous section.

3. Remove the corks from forked B♭, thumb B♭, and low C♯ bridge arms.

4. "Back off" the bridge adjusting screws on D, E, F, and A (Figure 38).

5. Replace the keys on the flute one at a time and re-seat* each one before installing the next, in the following order:
   a) G♯
   b) Trill keys (glued pads)
   c) G keys
   d) C (glued pad)
   e) F♯, F, E, and D
   f) A and B♭
   g) Low C
   h) Low C♯
   i) Low D♯

6. Follow standard pad clamping procedures.

7. Check the cup opening with the key opening tool. (Remove or add cork to the key foot as needed.)

**ADJUSTING
SCREW**

FIGURE 38
Adjusting the bridge screw

8. After all pads have been seated properly, adjust the bridge keys as described on pages 73, 74, Specific Woodwind Problems—Flute, Piccolo, Adjusting Bridge Keys.

Piccolo Padding

The piccolo repad* represents one of the most difficult of all repair problems. It is not advisable for the band director to undertake this task himself. As in dent work, soldering, etc., he should seek the advice of a local repairman if he considers it necessary to learn the skills needed for piccolo repadding.

Loose pads should be replaced in the following manner:

1. Replace the pad, as near as possible, in its original position.
2. Re-glue it with liquid shellac (tube) or,
3. Heat the pad cup with a small-tipped soldering iron.

    Note: Use of the bunsen burner on piccolo pads is apt to loosen and unseat the adjacent pads.

Except for other minor adjustments, piccolo repairs should be handled by a competent repairman.

Corking Tenons*
(List B Tools and Supplies)

1. Method A. This is the simplest and can be used satisfactorily on all tenons.
   a) Remove protruding keys.
   b) Remove the old tenon cork and the shellac with the hooked and straight scrapers.

←— CUT TENON CORK WITH THE GRAIN

FIGURE 39

   c) Measure the width of the tenon groove and mark the cork. (The grain of the cork should be parallel with the cut cork's length as in Figure 39.)
   d) Lay a straight edge on the marks and cut the cork with a bench knife or razor blade. (Cut the cork approximately one inch longer than needed.)
   e) Test the cork's size by placing it in the tenon groove.
   f) Bevel one end of the cut cork as in Figure 40.

BEVEL

APPLY CONTACT
CEMENT HERE

FIGURE 40
Beveling the tenon cork

g) Coat the *cleaned* tenon groove, the bottom side of the cut cork, and its beveled end with a thin layer of contact cement (see Figure 40).

h) Allow the cement to dry until it is no longer "tacky."

i) Press the beveled end of the cork into the tenon groove.

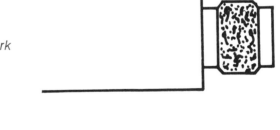

FIGURE 41
Beveled tenon cork

FIGURE 42
Sanding the tenon cork

j) Starting at the beveled end, press the cut cork firmly into the groove until it overlaps and makes a tight contact with the bevel.

k) Cut away the excess cork with a bench knife or razor blade.

l) Bevel the edges of the cork (Figure 41) with a file or a sanding stick.

m) Test the tenon for proper fit in its relative socket*.

n) If the joint is too tight, cradle the joint in the left hand (right handed person), palm up, with the left thumb on the tenon cork.

o) Insert a strip of garnet paper under the thumb and pull away briskly, simultaneously rotating the clarinet to the left to "sand off" the excess cork (Figure 42).

p) Repeat until the excess cork has been removed evenly around the tenon.

q) When a proper fit is obtained, grease the cork.

2. Method B. Although not necessarily better, Method B is preferred by many repairmen because it is much faster. It should, however, be used only on the small wood tenons (soprano clarinets and oboes) since shellac does not hold satisfactorily on many hard plastic instruments and on the large woodwind tenons.

a) Follow steps a) through f) of Method A.

b) Heat the stick shellac over the flame until it begins to melt.

c) Apply immediately to the cleaned tenon.

d) Repeat steps b) and c) until there is ample shellac to cover

SHELLAC SPATULA

FIGURE 43
Installing the cork with shellac

the tenon groove.

e) Heat the shellac spatula and smooth the shellac until there is equal distribution in the tenon groove.

f) Cradling the joint in the left hand as in n) above, melt the shellac in the groove with the heated spatula and immediately press the cork into the groove, beveled end first, with the thumb (Figure 43).

g) Continue until the cork is installed in the groove (Figure 44).

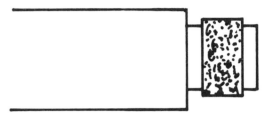

FIGURE 44
Tenon cork before beveling

h) Make sure that enough shellac coats the bevel so that a firm union is made with the overlapping cork.

i) With a bench knife, a scraper, or a screw driver, "flake away" the excess shellac.

j) Follow steps k) through q) in Method A.

Cleaning Fish Skin* Pads
(List A Supplies)

Sticking pads are most often caused by moisture accumulation on the pad skin. This is especially true when the player has consumed food or beverage containing sugar.

To clean, slip a piece of eyeglass cleaning paper over the tone hole, depress the pad lightly and pull the paper out slowly. Repeat the procedure until the pad is clean. For more stubborn accumulations, use a cloth saturated with alcohol.

Re-Bending Keys
(List A Tools)

Straightening bent keys involves a certain amount of risk, but the director should not hesitate if the bent key is functioning improperly.

Using the flat nose pliers, bend the key to the correct position. If a pad cup has been bent, use whatever tool is necessary to bend the cup, but avoid damaging the tone hole and pad. Check the pad seating with the feeler.

Replacing Flat Springs
(List A Tools and C Supplies)

1. Remove the key from the instrument.
2. Select a spring of the proper size and strength.
3. Unscrew the spring screws from the key and install the new spring.

   Note: On some saxophone models, the springs and screws are oversized, making it impossible to install standard flat springs. These models should be sent to a repairman.

Replacing Needle Springs
(List D Tools and Supplies)

1. If a spring has been broken off even with the post*, use the *broken* spring removing pliers (Figure 45).

FIGURE 45
Removing a broken spring

2. To remove a whole, but weak, spring, use the *whole* spring removing pliers (Figure 46).
3. Select the correct size spring by testing it in the hole.
4. Using the jewelers' anvil and the small end of the dent hammer, flatten the large end (flatten either end of a flute or piccolo *wire* spring).

   Caution! A needle spring held between two fingers while flattening might result in a punctured finger. Holding the needle spring by a pair of common slip-joint pliers is the safest means of preventing a dangerous ricochet.

FIGURE 46
Removing a whole spring

5. Insert in the post (about 1/16 inch of the flattened end should remain outside the post).

6. Using diagonal cutters (Figure 47), force the flattened end until it is even with the post.

7. Bend the spring so that it gives the proper key response.

   Note: Threaded springs are standard equipment on some brands of saxophones. Unless the director wishes to invest in a complete set of these springs, he should send the instrument to a repair shop.

FIGURE 47
Installing the needle spring

Removing Small Chips from Tone Holes (non-metal)
(List B Tools)

1. Remove the key from the instrument.

2. With the correct size tone-hole reamer between the first two fingers and thumb, *very lightly* twist the reamer to the right until the small chipped areas have been removed. Although this will somewhat alter the size and shape of the tone hole rim, it will allow a much better pad coverage*.

Repairing Large Chipped Areas in the Tone Holes (non-metal)
(List E Supplies)

1. Remove the key.

2. Clean the chipped area with alcohol.

3. Insert a tightly rolled piece of paper in the tone hole and let it unwind until it is against the inside of the tone hole walls (Figure 48).

FIGURE 48
Preparation for
tone hole patching

4. Mix a small amount of ebony compound as per directions.

5. With a small-bladed instrument, fill the cracked area and smooth out.

6. Allow twenty-four hours for drying.

7. Smooth the tone hole area with a flat file or a tone-hole reamer (depending on the type of tone hole).

8. Replace the key or ring, and test the pad for coverage* or clearance.

    Note: When chipped or uneven areas appear in metal tone holes and cannot be straightened with round nose pliers or releveled with the tone hole file, the instrument should be sent to a repairman, as it will probably be necessary to solder a thin strip of metal to the tone hole wall.

Re-Tightening Loose Tenon Rings
(List A Tools and Supplies)

If possible, this repair should be sent to a shop which has the proper, ring shrinking equipment. However, the following method, or similar methods, are acceptable substitutes.

1. Remove the ring and remember which edge will be replaced first (one end is sometimes wider).

2. Cut a narrow strip of waterproof paper to the ring groove's circumference.

3. Place the paper on the groove with the rough side against the wood.

4. Slip the ring over the paper (Figure 49). If extremely tight, tear ½ inch or so off the paper.

5. Tap the ring with the rawhide mallet until it is a distance of 1/16 inch from the groove shoulder.

6. Cut away the paper that is showing in the groove (Figure 49).

7. Tap the ring all the way against the shoulder.

8. Trim the remaining paper off the outside edge.

   Note: The large ring on the rim of the woodwind bell requires a shrinking die and cannot be properly tightened otherwise.

FIGURE 49
Tightening the tenon ring

◄— **CUT HERE**

Recorking Thumb Rests
(List A Tools and Supplies)

1. Remove the old cork and clean the surface.

2. Heat the thumb rest.

3. Apply a piece of treated cork.

4. Trim the excess cork.

5. Smooth with a sanding stick.

Loose Screws

Loose screws may be tightened or replaced with List A tools and supplies.

Repairing Stripped Threads (List E Supplies)

1. Remove the thumb rest or lyre socket.

2. Clean the screw holes with alcohol.

3. Mix a small amount of ebony compound and force into the stripped hole.

4. Replace the thumb rest or lyre socket.

5. *Push* the screw into the soft compound.

6. Let it dry for twenty-four hours.

Repairing Stripped Strap Rings (List E Supplies)

Follow the same procedure as In Stripped Threads.

Tightening Loose Posts (except metal woodwinds)

1. Method A (List A Tools and B Supplies)
   a) Remove the key(s).
   b) Remove the needle spring (Figure 46).
   c) Unscrew the post until it is halfway out of the body.
   d) Spread a small amount of powdered pumice around the screw (Figure 50).

FIGURE 50
Applying powdered pumice to the loose post

e) Re-tighten the post.

f) If the post is not solid, follow Method B.

2. Method B (List A Tools and C Supplies)

a) Follow steps a) and b) of Method A.

b) Unscrew the post from the body.

c) Slip one post shim over the threaded end of the post (Figure 51).

d) Replace the post.

e) If the post is still loose, follow Method C.

3. Method C (List A Tools and E Supplies)

a) Follow steps a) and b) of Method B.

b) Thoroughly clean the threaded section on the screw, as well as the portion inside the instrument body.

c) Mix enough of the ebony compound to fill any cracks or chipped-off areas around the post.

d) Fill the threaded hole and *push* while screwing the post into the hole.

e) Remove or smooth the excess compound.

f) Replace the key so that the post will be properly aligned.

g) Use a flute pad clamp (or a rubber band for a large bore instrument) to hold the key in place while drying (twenty-four hours).

h) Remove the key and replace the spring and key.

FIGURE 51
Post washer

POST WASHER

Occasionally a post will be so badly stripped that it will require a threaded post bushing or an inlaid piece of wood in the damaged area. In such case, refer the job to a professional repairman.

Removing Loose Action in Pivot Screws (all woodwinds) (List E Tools)

Constant use of a woodwind instrument eventually will cause loose action on pivot screw keys. The following procedure will remedy most of these problems.

1. Remove the pivot screw.

2. Select the correct size of countersinking reamer.

3. Insert the reamer in the pivot screw socket (Figure 52).

4. Twist to the right one-half turn, removing only a *small amount* of metal.

5. Test the pivot screw and key for tightness.

6. Repeat as necessary, *removing only a small amount of metal each time.*

FIGURE 52
Post reamer

Relieving Pivot Screw Pressure (List E Tools)

If the pivot screw has been countersunk too far, the key will bind when the pivot screw is inserted properly. The pressure can be relieved as follows:

1. Remove the pivot screw and key.

2. Using the proper size pivot screw reamer, remove a *small* amount of metal from the tapered hole in the key rod end (Figure 53).

3. Replace the key and test for free action.

4. Repeat as needed.

FIGURE 53
Pivot screw reamer

Relieving Hinge Tube Pressure (List E Tools)

If pressure exists between the end of the hinge tubing* and the post*, thereby causing slow action, follow this procedure:

1. Remove the hinge rod and key.

2. Using the hinge tube shortener (Figure 54), remove a *small* amount of metal from the end of the tubing.

3. Replace the key and hinge rod, and test.

4. Repeat as needed.

FIGURE 54
Hinge tube shortener

Eliminating Sluggish Key Action
(List A Tools and Supplies)

1. Check for loose or weak springs. If the spring is weak, bend it to the correct tension. For installing new springs, see General Woodwind Procedures—Replacing Flat and Needle Springs, page 61.

2. Check for dirty or rusted pivot screws* and hinge rods.*
   a) Unscrew the pivot screw or hinge rod one fourth of a turn and test the key.
   b) If the key operates freely, place a drop of oil on the contact points.
   c) Re-tighten the screw and test for freedom.
   d) If the key is still sluggish, unscrew the pivot screw, clean with a pipe cleaner, re-oil and tighten. If it is a hinge rod, remove it completely from the key, insert an alcohol saturated pipe cleaner through the hinge tube, clean the hinge rod, oil, and replace.
   e) If the key is not yet "free," proceed to the next test.

3. Check for a twisted post (wood or plastic instruments).
   a) Visually check the post's alignment with the key.
   b) If unable to detect visually, use the flat nosed pliers in a slight twisting motion on the post while operating the key. If this procedure reveals the problem, follow the Loose Post procedures for wood or plastic instruments, pages 65-66.

4. Check for bent posts *(metal instruments only).*
   a) Take a small block of wood or a wooden dowel and place it against the inside (key side) of the post.
   b) Using the rawhide mallet, tap *very lightly* against the post.

Caution: Do not use this procedure on wood or plastic instruments as permanent damage can occur to the delicate threads in the body.

5. Check for binding tone hole rings.

   If one of the rings is rubbing against the side of the tone hole, bend the ring with the flat nosed pliers.

   Caution: Do not use a screw driver with a prying motion against the tone hole wall. A broken tone hole is usually the result.

6. Check for bridge arm binding.
   a) Operate the sluggish key and inspect all moving parts.
   b) Bridge arms often bind against a post or against their relative bridge key.
   c) Bend the key arm slightly away from the obstruction.

7. Check for friction between the key (or its parts) and a loose pivot screw or hinge rod on an adjacent post.

   Note: If the above seven procedures have not solved the problem, the instrument should be sent to a repair shop. The problem is obviously in a bent body, a bent hinge rod, a bent hinge tube, or, on the flute, an accumulation of rust and grime inside the pinned hinge rod.

Removing Frozen Screws (List D Tools)

1. Saturate the pivot screw or hinge rod areas with penetrating oil.

2. Let it set overnight.

3. If the screw slot has been "wallowed out," saw a new (or deeper) slot in the pivot screw or hinge rod with the jewelers' saw (Figure 55). Although this may mean sawing slightly into the post, it will not ruin the post.

4. Exert heavy pressure and try to unscrew.

   Caution: Do not exert pressure with the screw driver towards the body or towards the hand which holds the instrument. A "slipped" screw driver can do serious damage to human flesh and muscle. Hold the instrument so that the screw driver will hit the work table, if it should slip (Figure 56).

5. Take the instrument to a repairman if the above procedure does not work.

FIGURE 55
Sawing a new slot

FIGURE 56
Removing a frozen screw

Repairing Worn Tenons

If a woodwind joint still wobbles after corking with extra thick cork, or if the tenon is chipped or cracked, the instrument should be sent to a repairman who is equipped to install tenon caps.

Removing Objects from "Stopped Up" Woodwinds (Flute and Trombone Cleaning Rods)

A broken swab, a pad, a ligature, a mouthpiece cap, or a can of cork grease often may become lodged inside the bore*. Usually these objects can be removed without trouble.

1. Oboe and soprano clarinet
   a) Insert a flute rod into the small end of the bore.
   b) Be careful not to damage the thumb or octave tube. Push firmly towards the large end of the bore.
   c) If firm pressure does not remove the object, *send it to a repair shop!*

2. Large clarinets and bassoon
   Use the trombone cleaning rod and repeat the steps in Number 1.

3. Saxophones
   a) Use the trombone cleaning rod and push the object towards the large end of the bore.
   b) If the object is a ligature that cannot be removed with a trombone cleaning rod, try jarring it loose by bumping the bell bow at the bottom with the heel of the hand.
   c) If neither method works, remove the key(s) near the lodged object and loosen it by reaching through a tone hole.

Repairing Broken Plastic Bodies

Many repair shops now have special cement that will mend any broken plastic instrument to complete satisfaction.

Refacing Mouthpieces

The need for a periodic inspection (at least once a year) of mouthpieces is often overlooked in clarinet and saxophone repairs. Even new mouthpieces will sometimes have warped rails which prevents good tone production. Players often complain that they can only find one or two good reeds in each box, when in reality, the "good" reeds just happen to be warped in the same direction as the mouthpiece rails.

Most repair shops have repairmen (or access to specialists) who can accurately reface a mouthpiece to any specification. During a slack season, every director should have a skilled mouthpiece repairman visit his band classes to check all clarinet and saxophone mouthpieces, and to reface those that are chipped or warped. An expert can service the entire clarinet and saxophone sections in one class period by taking one or two students at a time. The rehearsal can continue without serious interruptions.

Removing Chalky Deposits

Under no circumstances should an attempt be made to *scrape* away these deposits. A repairman has the proper chemicals to remove them without damaging the mouthpiece.

SPECIFIC WOODWIND PROBLEMS

FLUTE—PICCOLO

Replacing Head Corks
(List A Tools and C Supplies)

1. Remove the crown*.

2. Push the cork out the opposite (tenon) end (Figure 57).

FIGURE 57
Removing flute tuning cork

3. Remove the threaded disc from the screw end.

4. Remove the cork from the screw and save the cork for making trill key corks, key wedges, etc.

5. Clean the glue from the metal discs and from the screw.

6. Heat the disc that is permanently attached to the screw and coat the inside with white pad glue.

7. Immediately screw or push the cork against the melted glue and hold until cool.

8. Screw the threaded disc part way on, heat, and apply glue to its inside.

9. Immediately screw the disc up tight against the cork and hold until it cools.

10. Clean any excess glue and grease the cork.

11. Using a tuning rod, or wooden dowel rod, insert the cork (thread first) into the tenon end.

12. Push the cork into the joint until the ring on the tuning rod is in the center of the blow hole*. (See Figure 26, page 27.)

13. Test for leakage (page 28, Flute, Physical Inspection, No. 4) after replacing the crown.

Loose Foot Tenons
(List C Tools)

1. Place the base of the can opener type tenon expander in the vise.

2. Insert the tenon between the two rollers (Figure 58).

FIGURE 58
Expanding the foot tenon

3. Tighten the roller screw *lightly*.

4. Rotate the crank until the flute has made one complete revolution.

5. Remove the flute and test the tenon with the foot joint.

6. Repeat the above procedure, *gradually* increasing roller tension until a desired fit is obtained.

Adjusting Bridge Keys
(List B Tools and Supplies)

1. Thumb B♭. This problem is usually caused by a worn or missing cork on the small bridge arm.
   a) Determine the needed cork thickness by inserting various thicknesses of cork between the thumb key foot and the bridge arm.

b) Remove the A, B♭, and C keys and follow standard Key Corking procedures.

2. Forked B♭
   a) If the problem is missing or worn cork on the bridge arm, follow the key removal and adjusting procedures as listed in Repad, pages 55, 56, and standard Key Corking procedures.
   b) If the problem is a bent bridge arm, follow these procedures:
      (1) "Back off" the bridge adjusting screw on the F key (see Figure 38, page 56).
      (2) Using the flat nose pliers, bend the forked B♭ arm (near the G pad cup) until equal feeler* pressure is obtained between the F and B♭ pads.
      (3) Re-tighten the F bridge adjusting screw until equal feeler pressure exists on all three pads (F, F♯, and B♭).

3. Second and third finger F♯
   a) Loosen the third finger (D) bridge adjusting screw.
   b) Adjust the second finger (E) screw until equal pressure is obtained between the E and F♯ pads.
   c) Repeat the procedure to obtain equal pressure on the D and F♯ pads.

4. Low C and C♯
   a) If the cork is missing on the C♯ bridge arm, remove the keys and recork.
   b) If the C♯ bridge arm is bent, rebend the arm until equal pressure exists between C and C♯ when depressing the C key roller*.

Removing Loose Action From the Keys
(List A Tools and Supplies)

1. For loose action caused by missing foot cork (the foot or arm that touches the body when the key is open), follow standard corking procedures.

2. If the cork is intact, the loose action may be removed by gluing (with liquid shellac) a small square(s) of paper on the foot cork.

3. Although the key feet may be bent to remove the loose action, this technique requires much practice.

Removing "Clicking" From Keys
(List A Tools)

If the keys have been properly corked, the only remaining key noise is likely to be caused by the trill Bb arm (above the F♯ key) when fingering A, G, or G♯. Using the flat nosed pliers, bend the arm up slightly. If a slight bending does not eliminate the contact, the right hand key cups are opening too far and should have thicker foot corks.

Tightening the Head Joint Tenon
(List C Tools)

1. Tighten the flute head joint expander screw until the expander requires heavy, hand force to insert in the tenon end (Figure 59).

2. Make two or three turns.

FIGURE 59
Expanding the head tenon

3. Test the tenon for size in the socket* and repeat the above procedures, tightening the expander screw 1/16 turn each time until a snug fit is obtained.

Removing Head and Body Dents
(List E Tools)

1. Head joint dents
   a) Remove the tuning cork as described on page 72, Replacing Head Corks.
   b) Clamp the base of the head joint mandrel in the vise.
   c) Slip the head joint on the mandrel, tenon end first.
   d) Using the dent hammer, remove the dents.

2. Body dents
   a) Remove all keys as described on pages 55, 56, Flute Repad.
   b) Clamp the base of the body mandrel in the vise.
   c) Slip the body over the mandrel.
   d) Being careful to avoid tone hole damage, remove the dents with the dent hammer.

OBOE—ENGLISH HORN

Due to the intricate construction of the oboe and English horn, the director should restrict his involvement with them to care and maintenance, testing, and the simplest of repair problems. The flat and needle spring assortments, for instance, are not likely to have more than one or two sizes (or strengths) that are correct for the oboe. The pads are made of both skin and cork and are of special thicknesses, and many keys must be replaced simultaneously, etc.

If, however, the director wishes to attempt repairs, the following procedure is standard for the removal of the keys on most oboes.

Disassembling
(List D Tools and Supplies)

1. Remove the side B♭ key from the upper joint.

2. Remove the G♯ pivot screw*.

3. Remove the hinge rod* from the main line or stack*.

4. Unhook all springs from their spring blocks* and remove the keys. Be careful to place the screws and hinge rods in the mounting board and arrange the keys in their proper order.

5. Remove the two octave "teeter" keys (usually mounted with one hinge rod).

6. Remove the lower octave key.

7. Remove the upper trill key lever.

8. Remove the lower trill key lever.

9. Remove the two trill keys (one hinge rod).

10. Remove the left hand G♯ lever.

11. Remove the thumb lever.

12. On the lower joint, remove the hinge rod from the bottom of the long, low B♭ lever tubing.

13. Remove the pivot screw from the post under the B♭ spatula*.

14. Carefully remove the entire B♭ tubing mechanism from the body and from its linkage with other keys.

15. Remove the D♯ key.

16. Remove the forked F key.

17. Remove the B hinge rod (on the lower post).

18. Remove the pivot screw from the upper post on the B key.

19. Remove the pivot screw from the lower post of C.

20. Carefully remove the B, C, and C♯ keys.

21. Remove the trill key teeter*.

22. Remove the hinge rod from the stack keys.

23. Unhook the springs and remove the keys.

24. Remove the F♯ trill key.

From this point the director can perform most major repairs for which he has equipment. But it is advisable that no attempts be made at replacing cork pads, since they seldom deteriorate and are difficult to seat properly.

Leaking skin pads can now be replaced and seated individually with a minimum of interference from adjacent keys. Other problems (loose posts, broken springs, joint corks, etc.) should also be repaired while the instrument is disassembled.

Bridge keys may be adjusted with the adjusting screws, by recorking, or by bending as described in previous sections.

Assembling

To assemble, reverse the above procedures. Use caution to prevent bending the hinge rods and tubings.

SOPRANO CLARINETS

Disassembling
(List A Tools)

1. Remove the register key (upper joint).
2. Unscrew all side key hinge rods.
3. Remove the four side keys together.
4. Remove the thumb ring.
5. Remove the A♭ key.
6. Remove the A key.
7. Remove the stack* keys.
8. Remove the C♯-G♯ key.
9. Remove the E♭-B♭ trill key.
10. Remove the left hand levers (lower joint).
11. Remove the low F and G♯ hinge rod and keys.
12. Remove the low E key.
13. Remove the low F♯ key.
14. Remove the left hand low F lever.
15. Remove the ring keys.
16. Remove the B-F♯ trill key.

While disassembled, the clarinet should be thoroughly checked for loose posts, rusted or broken springs, chipped tone holes, uncorked keys, poor pads, etc. The hinge rods and tubes can also be cleaned and oiled.

Assembling

To assemble, reverse the above procedure. Oil all screws as they are inserted.

Installing Silencer Skins in Lever Keys
(List A Tools and Supplies)

1. Remove the left hand lever keys.
2. Wet the silencer skins and place over the lever pivots.

3. Push into the arm holes.

4. If there is still too much loose action, add extra skins.

Adjusting the A and A♭ Keys

Although some brands of clarinets have a flat area for cork on top of the A key, the cork will wear away so rapidly that it is futile to try to keep it corked. If the adjusting screw is set properly, there should be a minimum of noise without the cork. Use the feeler and adjust the screw accordingly.

Adjusting the Thumb Ring
(List A Tools and Supplies)

1. Check the thumb ring for level closing with the thumb tone hole while fingering F.

2. If the cork is missing or worn on the foot of the thumb ring or on the F key arm, re-cork as needed.

3. If the corks are intact but the thumb ring is out of adjustment with the F, bend the F arm up or down as needed. (This should be done *only* if the arm and foot are corked correctly.)

Adjusting the Key Rings
(List A Tools)

1. If the pads are of proper thickness, the key rings, when depressed, should be level with the tops of their respective tone holes.

2. Insert the pad slick between the ring and the tone hole, or between the pad and the tone hole (for bending).

3. If the pad closes first, place the pad slick under it. Reverse the procedure if the ring closes first.

4. Press lightly on the ring to bend.

5. Remove the pad slick.

6. The ring should now be even with the top of its tone hole when the pad is fully closed.

7. Repeat as needed.

   Caution: The use of a screw driver or another tool for the above procedure may result in punctured pads or in chipped tone holes.

Adjusting the Bridge Key
(List A Tools and Supplies)

The bent bridge key on the upper joint is a common problem. Not only will it prevent the use of forked E♭-B♭, but it will often bind on the C♯-G♯ key.

1. Check the under side of the upper bridge key for proper corking.

2. Cork with a thin cork if necessary. Since the upper bridge key rests on the lower joint bridge key, it is unnecessary to cork that part of the upper bridge which touches the body.

3. Bend the bridge key to its proper position, insert the lower joint, and test the two pads for unison closings.

Adjusting the Low E and F Bridge
(List A Tools)

On most clarinets the low F presser foot* (or crow foot) is rigid and rarely needs to be bent. Bend it if necessary, but if it shows *no* sign of being crooked, follow these procedures.

1. Test the two pads with a feeler for equal pressure.

2. If the low E is tighter, place the pad slick under the low E pad and bend the E spatula* down slightly.

3. Test, and repeat as necessary.

4. If the low F pad is tighter, hold the low E pad on its tone hole and lift its spatula lightly.

5. Repeat as necessary.

6. If there is loose action between the spatulas and the presser foot, press down on the spatula that is higher and bend the spatula arm (the arm that connects to the lever key) down as necessary.

   Note: Due to differences in the models and styles of various woodwind brands, the above woodwind repair procedures should be modified to fit the instrument. On some clarinets and saxophones, for instance, a set screw* locks the pivot screw* in position and must be unscrewed before removing the pivot screw. The director should check for the presence of other irregularities before beginning each repair.

Unsticking Tenons
(List A Tools and Supplies)

On new wood clarinets, the tenons will often swell and stick due to the absorption of moisture from playing.

1. Allow the clarinet to dry at room temperature so that the tenon will return to its normal size. (Sometimes it will take several days.)

2. Remove the tenon from the socket.

   Note: Most stuck tenons are caused by leaving the clarinet assembled after playing! If this is not the cause, proceed with step 3.

3. With a piece of garnet paper on the index finger, lightly sand the walls of the tenon socket.

4. Oil the bore and the socket with a good bore oil, or olive oil, and allow overnight drying.

5. If the tenon persists in sticking, send it back to the dealer or to a competent repairman who has the necessary equipment for accurate reaming and lathe work.

   Note: If a *real emergency* exists, the stuck tenon may be removed by inserting a knife blade or thin wedge between the joints and prying them apart. Be careful to avoid denting the ring and wooden shoulder.

Re-Setting the Octave (Register) Tube
(List D Tools and A Supplies)

If a leak has been found around the register tube*, follow these procedures:

1. Remove the register key.

2. Place one hand over the register tube while holding the upper joint.

3. Insert a large screw driver into the bore* and push upwards on the tube. This method works only on the tapered and unthreaded tubes. Do not attempt to remove a threaded tube, such as the oboe tube, in this manner.

4. Clean the outside of the register tube with waterproof or garnet paper.

5. Place the tube, large end first, on an awl.

6. Heat the tube and coat it with stick shellac.

7. While the glue is still in liquid form, push the tube into the hole.

8. When the shellac cools, flake away the excess shellac.

9. On most clarinets, the tube will protrude about 1/16 inch above the body.

10. Replace the register key and test for leaks.

ALTO AND BASS CLARINETS

Octave or Register Key Problems
(List A Tools and Supplies)

Register key mechanisms on bass and alto clarinets vary from a simple two key arrangement on the upper joint to an intricate maze of bridge rods and keys extending from the neck register key to the third finger, right hand. Therefore it is impractical to describe and illustrate the techniques necessary for adjusting all models.

If the model is the simple, vented pad (first finger, left hand) type, standard clarinet repair techniques will suffice.

If the model has an automatic register key mechanism, use the following points for determining the correct procedure for adjusting.

1. The lower register key should generally operate from third line B to fourth line D.

2. From fourth line E upwards, the upper key (usually on the neck) should open and the lower key should close.

3. Re-cork or bend the bridge mechanisms as needed for proper operation.

One-Piece Body Construction

The one-piece body on bass and alto clarinets is most practical and should be seriously considered when purchasing new instruments. A good alternative is to have the existing two-piece models made into one-piece models by a repairman. Although this also means purchasing a new case, the money and time saved on repairs will justify the conversion.

Disassembling
(List A Tools)

Follow the procedure given for soprano clarinets except:

1. Remove the third finger (left hand) hinge rod* and keys before removing C♯-G♯, and,

2. Remove the right hand stack keys in accordance with their design.

Adjusting the Bell Key
(List A Tools)

1. Check for correct corking.

2. Re-seat* the pad if needed.

3. Bend the key arm for unison closing with the low E and F keys.

Adjusting the Bridge Keys
(List A Tools and Supplies)

1. If the key felts are missing, install new ones with liquid shellac.

2. If the felt is intact, use the pad slick and bend the key arms for proper closings.

3. Test with a leak light.

4. If an individual pad is not seating* properly, heat with the bunsen burner and adjust as described on page 52, Seating Glued Pads (Except Saxophones).

BASSOONS

Though most problems of bassoon repair should be handled by a competent repairman, some can be managed by any director who has the time, skill, and patience.

Recorking the End Bow*
(List E Supplies)

If a leak has been discovered (by means of water stains or smoke leakage) around the flange* on the end bow, follow these procedures.

1. Remove the bow cap*.

2. Mark the end bow so that it may be replaced correctly.

3. Remove the two screws and the end bow, taking care not to destroy the gasket.

4. Using the old gasket for a pattern, make a new slightly over-sized gasket from the sheet of 3/32″ cork.

5. Thoroughly clean the end bow flange, and its corresponding surface on the joint, so that no grease or glue remains.

   Note: From this point, repair practices differ. Although use of the following method will mean that replacement of the gasket will be necessary whenever the end bow is removed, it offers a sure and safe way of sealing the end bow.

6. Coat the end bow flange, its corresponding surface on the joint, and *both* sides of the cork with contact cement.

7. After an ample drying time, place the cork on the end bow flange and press the cork against the flange thoroughly, so that the entire surface will adhere. Use a *clean* tool or wooden dowel rod end for pressing, so that no foreign matter will be left on the outer coated side of the cork.

8. Trim away the excess cork from the tubing and from the outside flange.

9. Observe the alignment marks (Step 2) and place the end bow on the joint.

10. With a wooden dowel or a screw driver handle, press the flange firmly against the joint.

11. Replace the holding screws.

12. Test for leaks.

If a hole is found in the tubing bow, or a leak around the metal collar that attaches to the wooden body, send the bassoon to the repair shop.

Repairing Stripped Threads
(List A Tools and E Supplies)

1. If the stripped threads are in the wooden body, install an over-sized screw or follow the procedure for Stripped Threads on page 65.

2. If the stripped threads are in a metal part, send the instrument to a repair shop that has the proper drills and taps*.

Re-Seating the Pads
(List A Tools)

Due to the construction of the bassoon, many keys cannot be heated, bridge mechanisms adjusted, nor pads tested for leaks, without first removing a key guard or an adjacent key(s). After removing the obstructing devices, re-seat the pads, adjust the bridge mechanisms, and test the keys for leakage as previously described on page 34, Physical Inspection, Numbers 5 through 8.

Re-Corking the Bocal*

Since the bocal cork is extremely close to the soldered nib*, inexperienced attempts at heating the bocal for re-corking could result in a loose and leaking nib. This process is best left to the experienced repairman.

SAXOPHONES

Adjusting the Octave Mechanism
(List A Tools)

1. If the octave mechanism does not function as described in Chapter 2 (Saxophone, Physical Inspection), page 36 (No. 4), check the octave bridge for damage (often caused by placing the instrument in the case without first inserting the end plug*).

2. Bend the octave bridge or re-cork as needed.

3. If the bridge key has not been damaged and the upper octave key remains open, bend the key as shown in Figure 60.

FIGURE 60
Adjusting the upper octave key

4. If the upper octave does not open when fingering upper A, reverse the procedure in Number 3 above.

5. Test.

Expanding the Tenon
(List C Tools)

When the neckpipe is loose in the tenon socket after the neck screw has been tightened, follow these procedures.

1. Place the base of the tenon expander in the vise.

2. Insert the tenon between the rollers (Figure 61).

3. Tighten the tension screw lightly.

4. Turn the crank until the neck has made one revolution.

5. Test the tenon for tightness in its socket*.

6. Repeat as needed, *slightly* increasing the tension screw pressure each time.

FIGURE 61
Expanding the neck tenon

Installing Key Bumpers
(List A Tools and Supplies)

1. Clean the felt receiving area.

2. Select the correct sized bumper and cut, if necessary, to the length that will produce the proper key opening.

3. Place a small amount of liquid shellac on, or in, the felt receiver and install the felt.

Figure 62
Type a felt holder

FIGURE 63
Type B felt holder

FIGURE 64
Type C felt holder

FIGURE 65
Type D felt holder

4. On Type D cups, it will be more convenient to remove the cups from the key guard for felt installation.

5. On Type B felt receivers, spread the tabs, cut the felt for size, insert the felt (gluing is optional), and bend the tabs to hold the felt.

6. On Type A key guards, more lasting results will be obtained by using contact cement.

Disassembling
(List A Tools)

The following procedures must be modified, when necessary, for each brand and model. Remove the keys in the following order:

1. Neck octave key

2. Octave bridge

3. Thumb key and lower octave key

4. Palm keys*

5. Side C

6. Side B♭

7. Low C and D♯

8. Upper stack* keys

9. Upper E

10. Teeter key

11. G♯ lever

12. Low C♯

13. Bell keys (B, B♭)

14. G♯ key

15. Lower stack keys

Disassembled, the saxophone can be scrubbed, tone holes can be leveled (D tools), keys can be corked, pads can be replaced, new springs installed, hinge rods and tubings cleaned and oiled, and individual pads seated without interference from adjacent pads.

To assemble the keys, reverse the above order.

Installing Neck Corks
(List C Tools and Supplies)

1. Remove the old cork.

2. Sand the cork area clean.

FIGURE 66
Heating the neck cork

3. Heat the neck and apply the stick shellac to the area to be corked. A thin layer should coat the entire area.

4. Install the neck cork while shellac is hot.

5. Wrap cotton cord around the cork (Figure 66).

FIGURE 67
Sanding the neck cork

6. Holding the cork protector over the neckpipe end, heat the neckpipe bore* with the bunsen burner (Figure 66), until the shellac is again melted. (The cork should twist easily on the neckpipe.)

FIGURE 68
Sanding the neck cork
(Optional)

7. Making sure the cork is in position, allow the shellac to cool.

8. Remove the cord.

9. Test the mouthpiece for correct cork size.

10. To remove excess cork, sand off as in tenon cork sanding (Figure 67) or as in a shoe shining motion (Figure 68).

11. The sides of finished cork should be *parallel* so that the mouthpiece will be snug when placed near the end. It will also enable the player to push the mouthpiece all the way up without cracking the mouthpiece. Only the saxophone with the tuning device needs to have a tapered cork.

Leveling the Tone Holes
(List D Tools)

Caution: If the unlevel tone hole has been caused by a body dent, *do not file* the tone hole until the body dent has been removed!

1. Remove the key(s).

2. Place the file on the tone hole.

3. While holding the file flat on the tone hole with the thumb (Figure 69), move the file "tang" in a sidewise motion (Figure 70).

FIGURE 69
Filing the tone hole

4. Continue the process until the tone hole is level, as evidenced by file marks on the entire tone hole rim.

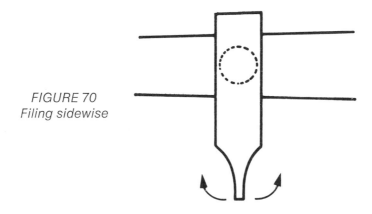

FIGURE 70
Filing sidewise

5. Replace the key(s) and reseat the pad.

Replacing Key Rollers*
(List D Tools and E Supplies)

If the key roller screw cannot be loosened in the conventional manner (Removing Frozen Screws, page 69), follow this procedure.

1. Remove the key or lever from the saxophone.
2. Break the roller tubing with the slip-joint pliers.
3. Using the slip-joint pliers, remove the frozen screw rod.
4. Remove the rust and plier marks from the screw rod.
5. Measure and cut a new roller.
6. Drill the roller to the screw rod size.
7. Bevel the edges of the roller.
8. Oil the new roller and place it on the key.

Tuning Mechanism Leaks
(List A Supplies)

Most saxophone tuning devices are constructed to precision, but the lubricant may dry or "break down" over a long period of time and allow minute leaks. If a smoke test reveals leaks in the tuning mechanism, follow these procedures.

1. Unscrew the mechanism from the neck.
2. Clean both parts with kerosene.
3. Apply a liberal coating of mutton tallow or good petroleum grease to the threads and tubing.

4. Replace the mechanism on the neck and remove the excess grease.

5. Test the neck for leaks.

Adjusting the Bridge Mechanisms
(List B Tools and Supplies)

If the bridge key cork is missing or worn, follow the standard key corking procedures (Corking Keys, page 50). Use the correct thickness of key cork. If re-corking is unnecessary, follow these steps.

1. Upper B
   Bend the B foot up or down as needed to close both keys together.

2. Upper C
   a) Check for a missing key felt.
   b) Bend the C arm or the C foot as needed to make the three pads close simultaneously.

3. G♯
   On most saxophones the G♯ lever spring is stronger than the G♯ key spring and works with an opposite or "overriding" action. If the lever does not close the key properly,
   a) Increase the tension on the lever key spring, or,
   b) Install a thicker cork on the bridge arm.

4. F♯ to G♯ bridge arm
   a) On saxophones with bridge adjusting screws, adjust the screw for unison closings of the F, F♯, and G♯ keys.
   b) On others, bend the bridge arm or re-cork until the three pads close together.

5. Forked B♭
   a) Bend the B♭ bridge arm (under the F♯ bridge arm) so that the F, F♯, and upper B♭ close simultaneously.
   b) Hold the G♯ lever down and check F, F♯, G♯, and upper B♭ for unison closings.

6. Second and third finger F♯.
   a) Check the second finger pad for unison closing with F♯.
   b) Check the third finger pad in the same manner.
   c) Check the second and third finger pads as in step 5. b) above.

   Note: On some older model saxophones a D♯ trill pad is operated by the second finger, right hand key. Some repairmen will permanently close them to prevent maintenance problems. If this pad is allowed to remain in operation, it should be adjusted to close simultaneously with the E, F♯, G♯, and upper B♭ key pads.

7. Low C♯
   a) On saxophones that have a bridge between low B and C♯, finger low C♯ and low B at the same time and check for unison closings.
   b) Adjust the bridge arm as needed.

8. Low B♭
   a) The low B♭ lever should also close the low B.
   b) If the two pads do not seat equally, re-cork (or felt) the table key* bridge, or bend the table key bridge, or bend the bridge mechanism that is located on the key rod or on the key cup.

9. As a final check, finger low B♭ and check for leaks in the G♯ key, since a leak in the G♯ often prevents good resonance in the bell key notes.

Re-Seating Pads

See Seating Glued Pads (Saxophones), page 53.

Repairing the Sticking G♯ Pad
(List B Supplies)

The G♯ pad on many saxophones often retains saliva or condensed breath moisture. Since the G♯ key spring is weak, the pad will sometimes fail to open when fingering G♯. One of two methods will probably eliminate this problem.

1. Clean the tone hole rim and the pad, and coat the pad with neatsfoot oil.

2. With a small cotton swab, apply a small amount of powdered pumice to the tone hole groove in the pad.

Silencing Special Keys
(List A Tools)

Some saxophones have special bridge arms and keys that cannot be corked conventionally. Figure 71 represents a typical bridge arm that fits into a fork or slot.

APPLY TAPE HERE

FIGURE 71
The special arm

1. Remove the lever from the saxophone.

2. Clean the prong.

3. Using plastic tape, wrap the prong until the correct thickness is obtained.

4. Remove the excess tape that protrudes beyond the prong end.

5. Test the prong in the fork or slot.

6. Replace the lever.

   Note: Silencer tubing is available from manufacturers for these special levers, but it is impractical for the director to purchase it in quantities.

Special Pads

Several brands and models of saxophones require special pads which are designed to give maximum resonance and intonation. Some models require special techniques for replacement and should be sent to a competent repairman. Others can be ordered through a dealer and installed by the director. In either case, replacement pads should conform to the original style, and should be installed without alteration of the pad cup*.

BRASSES

PISTON VALVE INSTRUMENTS

Removing Stuck Mouthpieces
(List A Tools)

Stuck mouthpieces occur more often than any other single brass repair problem. Consequently, more damage is done to mouthpieces and mouthpipes by unorthodox removal techniques than by any other brass repair attempts.

Although stuck mouthpieces can sometimes be removed by using pliers or a rawhide mallet, broken braces, twisted neckpipes, scarred mouthpieces, and ovalled shanks are often the results of such attempts.

A good mouthpiece puller can be purchased for less than the cost of replacing a mouthpipe and *should be standard equipment in every school that has a band program.*

1. Select the correct size of collar.

2. Place one collar in the bottom shoulder of the puller.

3. Place the mouthpiece and the mouthpiece receiver in the puller (Figure 72).

FIGURE 72
Pulling a mouthpiece

4. Place the second collar in the top shoulder of the puller.

5. Twist both screws *simultaneously* until the mouthpiece is free.

Refinishing Mouthpieces

Due to a variety of body chemicals, some individuals are allergic to brass. To prevent lip infections, the director should insist that all brass mouthpieces be replated when the plating has become worn or when the mouthpiece rim is dented or scarred. Since allergies sometimes include silver, having the mouthpiece re-plated with gold or nickel will often alleviate reactions.

Straightening Mouthpiece Shanks
(List B Tools)

1. Insert one jaw of the round nosed pliers into the shank (Figure 73).

2. Alternately grip the handles and rotate the mouthpiece to remove the dents.

3. Light "taps" with the dent hammer (List C tools) will permit more accurate dent removal.

FIGURE 73
Straightening the shank

Replacing Water Key Corks
(List A Supplies)

Replacing water key corks is very simple and should be a standard procedure for the director or for a student repair assistant.

1. Remove the old cork and the glue.
2. Select a *good* cork.
3. Place a small amount of liquid shellac on the small end of the cork.
4. Insert the cork in the cup and force it into place.
5. Slice or sand the cork until it seats* level on the nipple*.

Replacing Water Key Springs
(List D Supplies)

1. Remove the slide if the water key is on a removable slide.
2. Unscrew the axle or hinge rod*.
3. Remove the old spring.

4. Insert the new spring on or in the water key and replace it in the saddle* or yoke*.

5. Bend the spring ends around the yoke post.

6. Cut off the excess ends.

Pulling Stuck Slides
(List A Tools and Supplies)

1. Soak all areas (including the bore*) of the stuck slide with penetrating oil.

2. Let it set overnight.

3. Try to remove the slide in the normal manner.

4. If it is a main tuning slide with a large slide bow* and does not have a cross brace, *do not* attempt further action if it remains stuck. Send it to a repair shop!

5. If the slide has a cross brace on the slide tubing (do not confuse it with a cross brace on the sleeve*), tap the brace lightly with the rawhide mallet on the side that is stuck (usually the bottom). Repeated *light* tapping will, in many cases, unstick the slide. If not, send it to a repair shop.

6. If the stuck slide is one that has a small slide bow (first, second, or third valve slides), insert a tapered rod (i.e. a jaw of the round nosed pliers) against the inside of the bow, and tap with a rawhide mallet (Figure 74).

FIGURE 74
Removing the stuck small slide

Caution: Make sure that the tapered rod does not dent an adjacent tube, and that repeated tappings do not allow the instrument to slide off the holding mandrel onto the floor.

7. Small slides may also be removed by pulling on leather thongs, ropes, rags, and belts which have been inserted through the slide bow. But this often results in unsoldered joints, broken braces, and warped tubing. If the technique described in Number 6 above does not free the slide, send it to a repair shop.

Removing Frozen Valve Caps*
(List A Tools)

1. With a rawhide mallet, tap the sides and end of the valve cap.

2. Try to unscrew.

3. Repeat as needed, tapping with a little more force.

4. If the frozen valve cap is a top cap, damage can be done to the bell or neckpipe unless care is used when striking the the cap. To be safe, follow these procedures:
   a) Remove the bottom valve cap and the valve spring (if a bottom type).
   b) Remove the finger button.
   c) Holding the valve in the down position (Figure 75), tap down on the valve cap until it is lose.

FIGURE 75
Loosening a top valve cap

Removing Stuck Tuning Bits (Sousaphones)
(List A Tools)

1. Remove the mouthpipe from the sousaphone.

2. Tap the bit receiver* or ferrule* with the rawhide mallet.

3. Repeat as needed.

Freeing Stuck or Sluggish Piston Valves
(List E Tools)

1. Do not force the valve from the casing.

2. Pull the tuning slide on the stuck valve.

3. Check for the presence of foreign matter (a pencil, a piece of a flexible swab, etc.) by looking through the open tubing into the valve casing.

4. Check for a bent tuning slide (often caused by forcing books, gym shorts, etc. into the case).
   a) If a bent slide is evident, grasp the instrument firmly by the valve casings.
   b) With the fingers, pull the tuning slide back to its original position.
   c) Check the valve.

5. If the valve cannot be pulled from its casing by grasping the finger button (after overnight soaking with penetrating oil), the instrument should be sent to a repair shop.

   Caution: Do not try to "drive out" the stuck valve with a dowel or a similar round object. The bottom end of the *hollow* valve is sealed with a thin brass washer that will be ruined by such action.

6. If the valve is still tight but can be removed with normal finger pressure, check for dents in the casing.
   a) Use a valve cleaning rod and clean cloth to clean the casing.
   b) Hold the casing up to the light and locate the casing dent (usually a "bright" spot).
   c) Verify the dent by locating the dent on the outer case.
   d) Send the large brasses to a repair shop.

Note: Procedures e) through m) following are for cornets and trumpets. Only the director with considerable repair experience should attempt this procedure.

e) Adjust the reamer to the casing size by operating its top and bottom adjusting nuts simultaneously.

f) Place the square end of the reamer in the vise.

g) Holding the instrument with both hands, place the bottom end of the valve casing over the reamer and rotate slowly clockwise, keeping equal pressure on both hands.

h) If the reamer was set to the exact size of the casing, it will remove only the dent and will not mar the remainder of the casing walls.

i) Continue the clockwise motion until the reamer blades are visible on the above upper casing opening.

j) Remove the instrument in a slow, clockwise motion, keeping equal pressure on both hands.

k) Hold the casing to the light.

l) There should now be a slightly larger bright spot at the dent location.

m) Check the valve for freedom.

7. Check for gummy or corroded deposits on the valve.
   a) Using a non-abrasive metal polish, clean and polish the valve with clean cloths.
   b) Wash the valve in soapy water to remove the polish residue.
   c) Clean the valve casing.
   d) Oil and test the valve.

8. Check for the presence of filmy deposits.
   a) Inspect the valve ports* for the presence of a filmy build-up.
   b) Clean the valve and ports in soapy water.
   c) Clean the casing.
   d) Oil and replace the valve.
   e) If the valve is now free, clean the entire instrument to prevent a repetition of this problem.

9. Check for a binding valve guide.
   a) If the guide is one of the movable types, check for proper installation.
   b) If the guide is attached to the piston wall, check it for burrs.
   c) Unless the problem can be solved with minor efforts, send it to a repair shop. Damage to pistons can be caused by incompetent attempts to remove or replace the fixed guide.

Aligning the Valve Ports*
(List B Tools and A Supplies)

FIGURE 76
Alignment mark

Most piston* valve instruments have a line around the valve stem to indicate the correct open position. The line should be even with the top edge of the valve cap. (Figure 76.) The "down" valve position and the *unmarked* stem valves should be checked with a valve mirror.

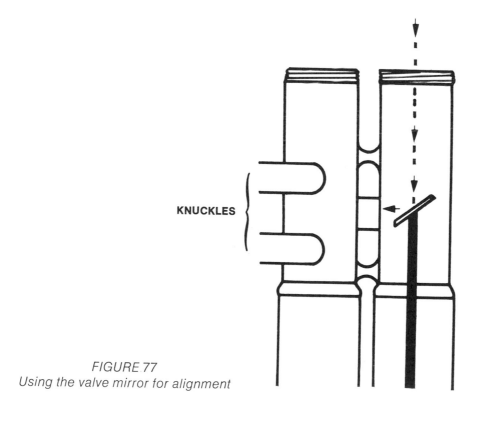

KNUCKLES

FIGURE 77
Using the valve mirror for alignment

1. Remove the piston adjacent to the valve being checked.

2. Insert the valve mirror (Figure 77) and check the ports in both "down" and "up" positions.

3. Add cork washers or felt washers under the valve cap* and finger button* as needed.

   Note: Valves with special corks and anti-click devices should be sent to a repairman who has factory parts.

Adjusting the Valve Spring Tension

A set of valve springs is inexpensive. For repair, the best solution is to buy and install new springs.

For instructions on temporary spring adjustment, see Emergency Repairs, page 121.

Removing Bell Tubing Dents
(List E Tools)

For removing dents that are located between the bell flare and the bell tubing curve, follow these procedures.

1. Clamp the large end of the tapered steel mandrel *tightly* in the vise.

2. Slip the bell over the mandrel.

3. With a rolling action, push out the dents.

4. Push out small, stubborn dents with the tip of the mandrel.

Removing Obstructions from Tubing
(List A Tools)

On the larger instruments these objects can usually be removed by rotating the instrument while jarring it with the hand. On smaller instruments a flexible rod must be used.

1. Pull all the affected slides.

2. Insert the rod in the small end of the bore.

3. Push towards the larger bore.

   Caution: Inserting the flexible rod through a valve casing can cause damage to the casing wall. If this procedure is necessary, the instrument should be sent to a repair shop.

4. A wedged coin can often pivot like a gate and allow the rod to pass through as though there were no obstruction. In this case, repeated movements of the rod will be necessary to remove it.

5. Strong water pressure from a flexible hose may also be used, especially on the larger brasses.

ROTARY VALVE INSTRUMENTS

Restringing the Valves
(List A Tools and Supplies)

1. Cut the string an inch or two longer than needed.

2. Tie a large knot in one end.

3. Insert the string through the hole nearest the key.

4. Wind the string around the post, and loop under the stop arm string screw (Figure 78).

FIGURE 78
Stringing the rotary valve

5. Check the key and make sure that it is level with the other keys.

6. Tighten the stop arm string screw.

7. Insert the string in the hole at the end of the key arm.

8. Loop the string around the string screw (See Figure 78).

9. Tighten the string screw.

10. Adjust for loose action as needed.

11. Remove the excess string.

Installing New Bumper Corks
(List A Tools and Supplies)

1. Remove the old cork.

2. Push the cork into the cork groove in the stop plate (Figure 79).

CUT OFF
EXCESS →
CORK HERE

FIGURE 79
Installing new bumper cork
(Side view)

3. Cut the cork off even with the top of the stop plate.

4. Remove the bottom valve cap.

5. Depress and release the valve key and check the alignment marks (See Figure 27, page 38).

6. Slice off the edge of the cork that contacts the stop arm (Figure 80) until the alignment marks coincide.

SLICE OFF HERE
TO ALIGN

STOP ARM

FIGURE 80
The rotary valve
(Top view)

Repairing Stuck Valves
(List A Tools and Supplies)

If a valve is stuck, *do not* try to unstick it by forcing the key down. Bent keys, broken strings, and "scored" bearings are often the results.

1. Remove the string.

2. Remove the valve cap.

3. "Back off" the stop arm screw about 1/16 inch (Figure 81).

4. Place the open palm under the valve to catch the bearing washer and valve.

FIGURE 81
The rotary valve
(Side view)

5. Tap lightly on the stop arm screw (Figure 81), until the valve is released.

6. Remove the stop arm screw.

7. Clean the stems and the bearing holes with a non-abrasive brass polish.

8. Wash the valve and the bearing holes with soap and water to remove the polish residue.

9. Oil the valve bearing points and replace in the casing with the long stem first.

10. Oil the bearing washer hole and place it over the stem and casing so that the casing and bearing washer marks are aligned (See Figure 27, page 38).

11. Use the rawhide mallet or a soft wooden block to tap the bearing washer evenly into the casing.

12. With the fingers, check the valve action by twisting the long stem.

13. Replace the valve cap.

14. Restring.

    Note: Do not attempt further repairs if the valve is not free. Send it to a repair shop.

Leveling the Keys
(List A Tools)

1. Release the pressure on the stop arm string screw.

2. Move the key to the desired position.

3. Tighten the stop arm string screw.

TROMBONES

Removing Stuck Tapers
(List B Tools)

On most trombones, the bell and slide sections join with a tapered tube* that is held together by a lock nut. Occasionally these will become

FIGURE 82
Removing stuck tapers

wedged. Do not exert excessive pressure in trying to release them. Broken soldered joints and twisted tubings can result.

1. Insert the wedges between the shoulders of the two joints (Figure 82).
2. Tap lightly until the joints separate.

Repairing Hand Slide Problems

1. Dented outer slides (List C Tools)
   a) Place the trombone slide mandrel in the vise and wipe it clean.
   b) Remove the outer (hand) slides and slip the dented slide over the mandrel.
   c) Using the small dent hammer, lightly tap on the edge of the dents.
   d) Test the slide for sticking.
   e) Repeat as needed.

FIGURE 83
Non-parallel inner slide

FIGURE 84
Bending the inner slide

2. Non-parallel inner slide (No equipment is necessary)
    a) Insert one of the inner slides into its companion outer slide, leaving the other inner slide free (See Figure 83).
    b) If the "free" inner slide is not parallel with its companion outer slide, grasp the "free" slide *near the cork barrel** and bend it until it is aligned properly with the outer slide (See Figure 84).

3. Non-parallel outer slides (List C Tools)
    a) Using the vernier caliper, measure the distance between the outer slides near the hand slide bow* and at the other end near the hand slide cross bar.
    b) If the slides are not parallel, use *only* hand or finger pressure to bend the bow in the direction necessary to make the slides parallel (Figures 85 and 86).
    c) Repeat procedure 2 above and re-align the inner and outer slides.
    d) If the slides still "bind," the problem is obviously in the soldered portions of the cross bar (send it to the repair shop) or in one of the problems to follow.

FIGURE 85
Narrowing the slide bow

4. Warped slides (A clean, flat table)
   a) Wipe the dust from the testing surface.
   b) Pull the inner slides free from the outer slides and lay on the flat surface. Note which side is off the surface.
   c) Using the hand and wrist, grasp the inner slides near the cross bar and twist in a direction opposite the warp (Figure 87).

FIGURE 86
Widening the slide bow

FIGURE 87
Removing warp from inner slide

d) Lay the slide on the surface and check.

e) Test the outer (hand) slides in the same manner on the flat surface.

f) To straighten the outer slides, grasp the slide bow in one hand and the slide cross bar in the other.

g) Twist *lightly* in a direction opposite to the warp (See Figure 88).

FIGURE 88
Removing warp from
outer slide

h) Test, and repeat as needed.

Caution: If the outer slide (hand slide) is badly warped, it should be unsoldered and re-aligned by a repairman.

5. Bowed slides (No equipment is necessary)

Note: Bowed slides often occur when a player inserts the tuning slide into the bell section while the trombone is "standing" on the slide bow knob. With a little patience and practice, the director can straighten the bowed slide without expense.

a) Remove the hand slide from the inner slides.

b) "Sight" down the slide towards the light to determine in which direction the slide is bowed.

c) Holding the slide rigid by the cross bar (hand slide bar), rest the slide bow knob on the end of a solid table or desk (Figure 89).

FIGURE 89
Straightening a bowed slide

d) *Lightly* rub the palm of the other hand over the bowed area.
e) "Sight" down the slide.
f) Repeat as needed until the slides appear to be straight.
g) Test the hand slide with the inner slides.

Note: Though procedures 1 through 5 above represent rather delicate repair techniques, the director who is conscientious and careful in his efforts can successfully eliminate many repair problems without costly mistakes.

6. Pitted stockings (List A Supplies)

Storing the trombone for summer vacations without proper *cleaning and drying* will often result in the formation of stubborn deposits and/or pitted areas on the stockings. Once this has happened, the player must contend with poor slides as long as he plays the instrument. The problem can be eliminated only by having new slides installed. A temporary but helpful remedy follows.

a) With a non-abrasive metal polish, clean the deposits from the stockings.

b) Using a rigid trombone cleaning rod (as described in Chapter I, "Trombone Cleaning," page 11), apply the polish to the end of the cloth and polish the inside of the hand slides; especially the bottom where the stockings are located when the slide is in first position.

c) Clean both the inner slides and the hand slides with soap and water and rinse thoroughly.

d) Since the pitted stockings will often give trouble when slide oil is used, cold cream and water should be used for more satisfactory slide action.

Freeing the Stuck Tuning Slide
(List A Tools and Supplies)

1. Saturate the inner and outer tubing with penetrating oil and let stand overnight.

FIGURE 90
Unsticking the tuning slide

2. Try to remove the slide as in Figure 90.

3. If the slide is not free, alternately tap on the ends of the cross bar (or brace) with the rawhide mallet until both slides are loose.

4. Polish the slides with a non-abrasive, brass polish.

5. Clean the slide with soap and water.

6. Grease the slides independently and in a spiralling motion coat each slide wall thoroughly.

7. Replace the tuning slide as in Figure 91.

Freeing the Stuck Valve

Follow the procedures for Rotary Valve Instruments, page 105.

FIGURE 91
Installing the tuning slide

Figure 92
Removing bumper cork

Replacing Slide Bumper Corks
(List E Tools and Supplies)

1. Unscrew the slide locking arm from the cork barrel.

2. Slip the cork removing tool over the inner slide and push its hooked tip into the cork barrel (See Figure 92).

3. Twist the tool to the right while simultaneously pulling away from the cork barrel.

4. Repeat Number 3 above until *all* cork (sometimes felt) is removed.

5. Cut a strip of 3/32 inch cork the same width as the old cork.

6. Using the dent hammer and jewelers' anvil, hammer the cork to make it supple.

7. Wrap the strip of cork around the slide, cut it to length, and insert it in the cork barrel.

8. Use the butt end of the cork removing tool to push the bumper to the bottom of the cork barrel.

9. Test with the slide lock for correct thickness.

10. Repeat the above procedures for the other slide.

PERCUSSIONS

DRUMS

Installing New Heads

When new heads are to be installed on a bass drum, timpano, snare drum, timbale, conga, tom-tom, cocktail drum, or bongo, a few basic steps should be followed.

1. Release the tension on the screws (one turn per screw) in a clockwise motion around the drum.

2. Check the rim for cuts, dents, and raised wood grain.

3. Sand the rim with a fine garnet or waterproof paper.

4. Coat the rim lightly with paraffin, graphite, or powdered talc.

5. Grease the tension screws lightly with mutton tallow or a light petroleum grease.

6. Check the hoop for dirt and rough areas.

7. Place the hoop on the drum and, in a clockwise motion, tighten each screw, one turn at a time.

8. Check the head to see that it is level.

9. Test the head near each screw for tuning.

Installing New Hardware

New lugs, mufflers, snare butts, drum key holders, and accessory brackets can be purchased for all brands of percussions, and they are easily installed.

1. Remove one of the heads.

2. Remove the old device (if replacing) by unscrewing it from inside the shell.

3. Install the new device, making certain that the mounting screws are equipped with lock washers and are tightened snugly.

4. For installing a new device, locate the desirable position for it on the shell, then mark and drill the holes.

5. Install as in Number 3 above.

MALLET INSTRUMENTS

Replacing Worn Glockenspiel Grommets*
(List A Tools)

New grommets can be purchased through a local music dealer or direct from the factory. Bent or worn bar* retaining screws and new backing felt, if needed, should also be ordered at the same time.

1. Remove the screws from each bar. Some bar retaining screws have a three-way locking security—two lock nuts plus a threaded hole in the mounting rail.

2. Clean the mounting rail or backing felt.

3. Check the mounting rail for looseness against the frame.

4. Clean each bar.

5. Replace and check each bar.

Other Mallet Repairs

Major repairs on other mallet instruments should be left to the factory. The only exception is the replacement of drive belts when a list of factory instructions is available.

CYMBALS

Cracked cymbals can be repaired to give temporary service.

1. Drill a hole at the end of the crack.

2. Saw away the portion as in Figure 93.

3. Smooth the edges.

FIGURE 93
Repairing a cracked cymbal

SAW OUT
DOTTED AREA

SUMMARY

Many problems that occur in an average band have been omitted from this chapter because the necessary equipment and repair skills are not available to most band directors. The following repairs should be handled only by a competent repairman who has the proper equipment.

1. Unsoldered braces
2. Broken keys
3. Broken tenons
4. Broken woodwind bodies
5. Cracked woodwind bodies
6. Major dents
7. Key swedging
8. Burnishing
9. Shortening clarinet barrel joints
10. Installing tenon caps
11. Installing floor pegs on bass clarinets
12. Tenon reaming
13. Mouthpiece re-facing
14. Buffing
15. Lacquering
16. Major work on piston or rotary valves
17. Timpani pedal repairs
18. Making hinge rods
19. Straightening hinge rods
20. Un-pinning flute hinge rods
21. Acid cleaning mouthpieces
22. Pickling* brass instruments
23. Removing lacquer
24. Removing threaded octave tubes

5

Emergency Repairs

Occasionally, just prior to a performance, a director will be faced with repair problems that cannot be solved through the use of standard repair practices due to time limitations. In such cases he must take stopgap measures to make the instrument play.

The simplest solution is to have the student borrow an instrument from a band member in a different performance group. A change in instruments is not apt to mar the over-all performance except where the student has prepared a solo.

Other corrective measures are listed below but these are only *temporary*. Following the concert or performance, the instrument(s) should be repaired properly, either by a competent repairman or by the director, using the techniques described in the "Standard Repairs" chapter.

It should be noted that in addition to the following list, many of the techniques given in the "Standard Repairs" chapter can be used effectively for emergencies.

WOODWINDS

Loose Pad

Since there will normally be enough glue left in the cup, place the pad in the cup and heat the cup with a match or cigarette lighter until it sticks.

Split or Leaking Pad

Cut a piece of transparent mending tape to the size of the pad. Place the tape over the tone hole with gummy side up, and press the key.

Loose Tenon (non-metal)

Wrap dental floss, thread, cotton string, French horn valve cord, paper, or tape around the tenon and grease.

Loose Tenon (metal)

Wrap one layer of transparent tape around the tenon.

Undersized Saxophone Cork

Wrap the cork with paper or tape until it is large enough for proper tuning.

Broken Spring

Whether the spring is flat or of the needle type, a rubber band can be effectively employed to make the key function properly. Be careful not to bind or hinder the action of an adjacent key.

Loose, Bridge Adjusting Screws

Set the adjusting screw for the proper bridge action and place a drop of clear fingernail polish on the screw head.

Loose Thumb Rest

Use transparent tape to hold it on the body.

Loose Key Guard (bassoon and saxophone)

Using a piece of French horn valve cord, tie the guard flange down against the body.

BRASS

Leaking Water Keys

Using a rubber band, loop it on the water key just above the cork.

For missing corks, use a piece of adhesive tape across the nipple*.

Unsoldered Braces

Wrap several strands of French horn valve cord around the solder flange* and tighten snugly against the tubing.

Unsoldered Finger Hooks

Use French horn valve cord and transparent tape to attach the finger hook in position.

Leaking Tubing

If acid holes have been discovered, use transparent tape for patching.

Leaking Soldered Joints

1. Clean the area.
2. Apply contact cement or clear fingernail polish to the leak.

Extremely Loose Second Valve Slides (cornet and trumpet)

Use a rubber band by looping around the pull knob* and the valve casing*, or seal each joint with transparent tape.

Repairing Valve Springs

Stretch the springs if they are weak. Cut off one or two loops if they are too strong, and bend the severed end coils until the spring will stand erect when placed on that end.

Broken, French Horn Valve Spring

Loop a heavy rubber band, or several small ones, over the valve cap and under the valve key.

Missing String Screw on French Horn Key

Pass the string through the threaded hole on the lever arm and tie it securely.

If the missing screw is on the stop arm, use the string screw from the lever arm on the stop arm, and tie the string to the lever arm.

Missing Water Key Screw, Hinge Rod, or Pivot Screw

Use a round toothpick for an axle or pivot point.

SNARE DRUM

Broken Heads

Keeping spare heads is the only sure solution.

INSTRUMENT CASE

Broken Handle

Make a handle with a coat hanger, pad with rags or paper, and wrap with friction or plastic tape.

Broken Latches or Hinges

Use a belt or rope to loop around the case.

6

Terminology*

Since a *complete* list of terms used in the repair industry would be of no practical value to the band director, and since repair jargon varies geographically, the following list contains (with a few exceptions) only the generally accepted terms with which the average director or instrumentalist will come in contact. While many terms will seem elementary or unnecessary to some readers, they will prove beneficial to others.

No attempt has been made to give prices on repair items, nor to make definitive statements regarding repair practices. Price changes are frequent throughout the instrument industry, and repair philosophies vary from city to city.

BALANCER: The weight attached to a trombone tuning slide which helps overcome the leverage produced by the hand slide*.

BAND: 1. A metal ring that is compressed into a pre-cut groove on a cracked woodwind to prevent the crack from widening. 2. The repair of a cracked woodwind, e.g. "to band."

BAR: A metal or wood tone block common to all keyboard type percussion instruments.

BEARING WASHER: A thick washer with an extended, tapered hole, through which the stem of a rotary valve* is inserted.

BELL BOW: The final, large, curved tubing preceding the beginning flare of the bell.

BELL SCREW: A screw that holds the bell of a brass instrument in position.

BELL SPUD: A small, round nut* attached to a flange* which receives the bell screw*.

BLOW HOLE: The opening in the lip plate of a flute or piccolo into which air is blown to produce sound.

BOCAL: A bassoon neckpipe* or crook*.

BORE: 1. The opening in all wind instruments through which

*For the reader's convenience, terms from this chapter will be identified by an asterisk in all chapters, wherever they first appear.

the sound waves pass. 2. The size of such openings.

BOTTOM CAP: See End Bow.

BOW: The curved tubing on brass and woodwind instruments.

BOW CAP: The protector cap that fits over the end bow* on a bassoon butt joint*.

BOW KNOB: The knob which is soldered to the small bow* on brass instrument slides to facilitate removal of the slides.

BRIDGE: See Yoke.

BRIDGE KEY: A woodwind key containing a special arm which actuates another arm for opening and closing key cups* simultaneously.

BUMPER: The felt, cork, plastic, or rubber attached to keys, levers*, braces, slides, or finger buttons to prevent a metallic "click" when actuating the moving parts.

BURNING IN: Heating the pad cups* on a woodwind key while depressing the key in order to seat* the pad correctly on the tone hole*.

BURNISH: The use of a smooth, file-shaped tool to "rub out" dents on brass instruments— especially on the bell part— and to polish plated instruments where buffing is impractical.

CASING: The walls of a piston* or rotary valve*.

CHAMBER: 1. The resonating section of a woodwind mouthpiece. 2. Sometimes used synonymously with "bore."*

COLOR BUFF (or COLORING): After overhaul, the final buffing with jeweler's rouge of a brass instrument which produces a "mirror" finish.

CORK BARRELS: The large sleeves* on the upper ends of the inside slides of trombones that contain corks or springs against which the hand slide* bumps.

COVER: Used to denote how the pads on a woodwind instrument seat* on the tone holes. If pads are said to "cover" well, they fit evenly and allow no leaks.

CRACK WIRE: See Pin.

CROOK: 1. Usually, the mouthpipe* of a bassoon. 2. Occasionally used synonymously with slide bow*.

CROW FOOT: Same as Presser Foot.

CROWN: The cap or button that is attached to the tuning cork* of a flute or piccolo head joint*.

DEGREASER: A solution which removes buffing compounds from the instrument prior to lacquering*.

DIE: A tool for making threads on the outside of a rod.

DING UP: A colloquialism meaning to do only the needed repairs to make an instrument play. Often used synonymously with "playing condition."*

DIP: A solution that cuts grime and tarnish from the interior tubings of brass instruments, leaving them with a "new" finish. Most dips can be used without harming the lacquer finish. Some repairmen, when referring to dip, precede it by using the commercial brand name.

EMORY BUFF: The process of buffing with an emory compound*.

EMORY COMPOUND: A buffing compound that is coarser than tripoli* and used in polishing badly pitted instruments.

END BOW: The metal bow* or curved tubing with an attached flange* that connects the two bores* at the bottom of the butt joint* on a bassoon.

END CAP: See Bow Cap (bassoons).

END CAP: See Tenon Cap (woodwinds).

END PLUG: A plug inserted in the small end of a saxophone (where the mouthpiece fits) to prevent bending the octave bridge* when the saxophone is placed in the case.

FEELER: A small dowel (about the size of a wooden match) with a thin strip of cellophane attached to one end. It is used to locate light or heavy pressure areas on woodwind pads.

FERRULE: A short, sometimes ornate, tube that connects two longer tubes or sleeves*.

FINGER BUTTON: A pearl-topped cap that is screwed into a piston* valve stem*.

FINGER HOOK: A hook for the little finger (right hand) on cornets or trumpets and for the

little finger (left hand) on French horns, which assists the player in locating and keeping the proper hand placement on finger buttons* or levers*.

FINGER RING: A ring (sometimes adjustable) on the third valve tuning slides of cornets and trumpets, by which the player adjusts the slide for proper intonation.

FISH SKIN: The thin, translucent skin that is used to cover clarinet, oboe, flute, and piccolo pads, and oboe reeds. It is also used to insert between pivot joints in levers*.

FLANGE: The thin, metal part (usually diamond or oval shaped) on the end of a brace, lyre holder, bell spud*, or water key saddle*, etc. which acts as a broad holding surface when soft-soldered to an instrument body.

FLAT SPRINGS: The springs mounted on woodwind keys by a small screw(s).

FLUSH BAND: The metal ring which is compressed into a pre-cut groove in wooden instruments to prevent further cracking.

FLUTE PAD WASHERS: Paper washers (or shims) of varying diameter and thickness that are placed in the flute pad cup to allow proper seating* of the pad.

FOOT JOINT: The short, lower joint on a flute containing the low C, C♯, and D♯.

GOLDBEATER'S SKIN: See Fish Skin.

GOOSENECK: A term used by some manufacturers and repairmen to denote the curved tubing that extends between the neckpipe* and main tuning slide or first valve casing of a sousaphone. The term is also applied, by some, to any tube* with a double curve.

GROMMETS: Rubber or leather cylindrical washers mounted over a retaining screw on a glockenspiel bar*.

HAND SLIDE: The movable, outer slides of a trombone containing the slide bow* and water key.

HARD SOLDER: Same as Silver Solder.

HEAD JOINT: The upper joint on a flute or piccolo.

HEAD JOINT CORK: Same as Tuning Cork*.

HINGE ROD: A long screw, varying in length, which acts as a bearing for the hinge tube* attached to keys on woodwinds. Each end of the screw is mounted in posts*.

HINGE TUBE: The hollow tube that forms part of a woodwind key, into which the hinge rod* is inserted.

INTERNAL CLEANING: A brass instrument term used by many repair shops denoting the removal of all slides, valves, and water keys, immersion in a soap solution, scrubbing tubing interiors with brushes, rinsing and re-greasing slides and valve caps. Though practice varies from shop to shop, new corks and felts and valve alignment are often included.

JOINT CAP: Same as Tenon Cap.

JOINT COVER: Same as Tenon Cap.

JOINT LOCK: A mechanism for holding two woodwind joints (specifically bassoons) in proper position after assembling.

KEY CUP: The cup attached to woodwind keys that hold the pad.

KEY GUIDE: A U-shaped metal tab which guides a long woodwind key back into correct position on its tone hole* when the key is released.

KEY ROLLER: The mother of pearl (or plastic) tubes on woodwind keys that provide a smoother, more rapid change of finger positions.

KNUCKLE: The short, curved tubing attached to the valve casing, onto which the tuning slide sleeves* are soldered.

LACQUER: 1. The clear liquid that is sprayed on instruments after polishing to prevent tarnishing. 2. The process of lacquering, i.e. "to lacquer."

LAPPING: A process of polishing (or honing) brass instrument valves with pumice and oil, whereby the valve is pushed, pulled, and rotated in the valve casing, or in a "lapping block," to insure precision fitting.

LEAK LIGHT: A device for detecting pad leaks in woodwind instruments when the keys are closed.

LEVER: 1. A woodwind key without a pad cup, usually operating on a fulcrum. 2. Any arm that actuates another moving part (i.e. the valve lever on a French horn).

LIP PLATE: The attachment on a piccolo or flute head joint* on which the lower lip is placed.

LOCK PLATE: A small plate attached to the body of some woodwind instruments which prevents the post* from turning.

MANDREL: A wooden or metal rod, sometimes tapered, to hold instruments in a vise while cleaning, soldering, etc. —or a rod utilized as a "backup" while removing dents by burnishing*.

MOUTHPIECE RECEIVER: A small ornate tube (or ferrule*) which reinforces or strengthens the mouthpipe* where the mouthpiece is inserted.

MOUTHPIECE: The tubing into which the mouthpiece is inserted in brass instruments, or onto which the mouthpiece is placed on woodwind instruments (neckpipe*).

MUTTON TALLOW: The rendered fat from sheep. Most meat departments will give this tallow to customers at no charge. It can be cut into small chunks and slowly melted in a skillet. When the melting action is completed, the tallow should be poured into its final container. When cooled, it forms a white paste similar to cork grease.

NECKPIPE: The curved metal tube* on saxophones and large clarinets into, or onto, which the mouthpiece is placed. Bassoon bocals* are also referred to as neckpipes*.

NEEDLE SPRINGS: The needle-like springs which are mounted in woodwind posts* (or, in rare cases, mounted on a key).

NIB: The small, nipple*-like tube* on a bassoon bocal* that contains a vent hole for the whisper key*.

NIPPLE: A small, round piece of metal (soft soldered to tubing) on which the water key cork seats*.

NUT: A round (usually knurled), square, or hexagonal piece of metal which contains a threaded hole.

OCTAVE BRIDGE: The mechanism on a saxophone (usually protruding beyond the tenon receiver*) that actuates the upper octave key on the neckpipe*.

OCTAVE TONE HOLE: Octave Tube.

OCTAVE TUBE: The tube* inserted through the body of woodwind instruments, especially at the octave or register key and the thumb, to prevent moisture from clogging the opening.

OVERHAUL: The most complete repair of an instrument. The following items are generally included:
A. Woodwinds:
1. All keys and levers are removed from the instrument

body. On metal woodwind overhauls, springs are also removed. 2. Thorough cleaning of body parts, inside and out (the lacquer is removed on brass saxophones). 3. Body parts are polished (dents in metal woodwinds are removed and brass-finished saxophones are also lacquered*). 4. All joints, neckpipes, or tenons* are recorked and refitted. Some repairmen do not remove tenon corks if they are new or in good condition. 5. Trademarks are re-gilded or re-silvered, or new decals are placed on some plastic instruments. 6. All keys and levers are polished (brass-finished saxophone keys are also lacquered*). An extra charge is usually made for replating nickel or other plated keys which have become worn from use. 7. New bumper* corks are installed on all keys. 8. Old pads are removed and replaced with new pads (the only exception being that *good* cork pads on oboes and clarinets are usually left intact since cork does not deteriorate like skin pads). 9. Rust and gummy solutions are removed from hinge rods* and hinge tubings*. 10. Hinge rods*, hinge tubing*, and pivot screws* are oiled. 11. New silencer skins* are installed in levers*. 12. All pads are seated for proper coverage*. 13. Loose action is removed from worn keys. 14. All loose posts* are tightened. 15. Loose bell and tenon* rings are tightened. 16. Bent keys and levers* are straightened. 17. Broken or rusted springs are replaced. 18. Bassoons: a new gasket is installed on leaking end bow*. 19. Flutes and piccolos: new head joint corks are installed. 20. Tone hole* "nicks" and "chips" are removed. 21. The instrument Is thoroughly checked for proper mechanical operation and intonation. *Note:* Again, repair shop practice varies according to the seriousness of additional repair problems and the overhaul price. But other items which should be included on an overhaul are: silver soldering broken parts, installing tenon caps*, repairing or replacing cracked tone holes, shortening joints, re-facing mouthpieces, etc.

B. Brasses:

1. All slides, valves, water keys, tuning mechanisms, and valve caps are removed. 2. Lacquered instruments are placed in a solution for removal of old lacquer. 3. Interior is cleaned and scrubbed thoroughly. 4. Broken, leaking, or loose parts are soldered. 5. Accessible parts of the entire instrument (including screws) are rough buffed* with an emory* or tripoli* compound. 6. All dents are removed. 7. All parts of the instrument are pickled* or dipped*. 8. Pits in the instrument caused from body acids are removed (unless too deep) by sanding, emory buffing*, strapping*, and by a second rough buffing* with tripoli*. 9. Parts of the instrument not rough buffed* are ragged*. 10. Instrument is buffed with white rouge. (This step is omitted by some shops.) 11. Bell interior is polished as deeply as practical. 12. The instrument and parts are color buffed* or rouged*. 13. Instrument is placed in degreaser*, cleaned, and dried. 14. All instrument parts are

lacquered*. 15. Instrument is then re-cleaned inside to remove buffing and lacquer dust. 16. Slides and valve caps are greased, new felts and corks installed (new strings on French horns), and valves are properly aligned and oiled. *Note:* The finishing treatment for plated instruments varies. Plated instruments with smooth finish are burnished* and color buffed*; satin finished instruments are burnished* and scratch brushed; neither is lacquered* except by special request of customer.

PAD CUP: Same as Key Cup.

PAD SCREW: The metal screw that fits through the pad washer* on flutes.

PAD SPUD: A small, threaded, metal tube or disc that is soldered into the bottom of a pad cup* to receive the pad screw* (most flutes and some saxophones).

PAD WASHER: A small metal disc which holds the flute pad in place.

PAPER WASHERS: Washers of varying diameters and thicknesses placed under flute pads to insure proper seating*.

PALM KEYS: The keys on a saxophone operated by the palm of the left hand (upper D, D♯, and F).

PICKLE: An acid solution in which instrument parts are immersed for cleaning.

PIN: 1. A small threaded rod that is screwed into wooden instruments to prevent cracks from widening. 2. The repair of a cracked woodwind—i.e. "to pin."

PIN VISE: A pencil-like device for holding needle springs*.

PISTON: The valve part that operates vertically with a pumping motion inside the valve casing.

PIVOT SCREW: The short screw mounted in posts* on woodwind instruments on which the key turns or pivots.

PLAYING CONDITION: The third most complete repair of an instrument, following (1) overhaul* and (2) repad* (woodwinds) or internal cleaning* (brasses). For woodwinds: to install new pads where needed, straighten bent keys, recork joints or keys where needed, re-seat leaking pads, solder broken keys, replace broken springs, and remove key noises, etc. For brasses: re-soldering loose parts, pulling stuck mouthpieces, removing accessible dents, pulling and greasing all slides, replacing bad water key corks, and "freeing up" valves. Some repairmen use the term interchangeably with "ding up" and "internal cleaning."

PORT: An opening in a piston* through which the tone passes.

POST: The knob-like part mounted to the body of a woodwind instrument which holds the pivot screw* or hinge rod*.

POST LOCK: A device for preventing a woodwind post* from turning. It can be one of several devices—a set screw*, lock plate*, etc.

PRESSER FOOT (frequently called "crow foot"): The part of a woodwind key against which another key or bridge presses to operate both keys simultaneously. Specifically, the forked arm on the clarinet low F.

PROTECTOR CAP: The removable cap at the base of a bassoon butt joint which protects the end bow* from damage. Sometimes used, erroneously, for Tenon Cap*.

PULL KNOB: Same as Bow Knob*.

PULL RING: On French horns, the ring which is soldered onto the slide bow* to permit easy removal of the tuning slide.

PUMICE: A fine abrasive powder used in lapping*, strapping*, polishing and tightening loose posts.

RAGGING: A process of using a rag, saturated with polish, in a "shoe shining" motion to produce a glossy finish around valve casings and tubings that cannot be reached with a buffing wheel.

REAMER: A drill-like tool for enlarging holes, which leaves a smooth finish for precision fittings. Often used on out-of-round or dented valve casings prior to lapping*.

REGISTER TUBE: Same as Octave Tube*.

REPAD: (Woodwinds only): The second most complete repair of a woodwind instrument. Generally, to remove all old pads and replace with new ones. Specifically: 1. Remove all keys from the instrument. 2. Clean the instrument body parts. (Plastic and metal woodwinds can be scrubbed with soap and water.) 3. Clean all keys. 4. Straighten bent hinge rods*, tubings* and keys. 5. Clean rust and gum from *all* hinge rods and tubings, and oil. 6. Remove *all* old pads and replace with new ones, preferably double skin pads. Exception: cork oboe and clarinet pads in good condition should be left untouched. 7. Replace missing bumpers*. 8. Repair chipped tone holes*. 9. Seat all keys for proper coverage*. 10. Install new fish skins* in lever* pivot points. 11. Pickle the mouthpiece. 12. Test for leaks and for correct key action.

Note: Although an additional charge will be made by most repairmen, bad tenon* corks, loose posts*, broken springs, and loose key action should be remedied while being repadded to prevent additional trips to the repair shop.

ROTARY VALVE: A type of valve (such as on the French horn) with a rotating motion, as opposed to the "pumping" action of a piston* type valve.

ROUGE: 1. A red polishing compound used in color buffing*. 2. The process of color buffing, i.e., to "rouge" an instrument.

ROUGH BUFF: The use of tripoli* on a buffing wheel which removes tarnish during the first buffing process.

ROUGING: Same as Color Buffing.

SADDLE: 1. Same as Yoke*. 2. Sometimes used in referring to the thumb saddle*.

SCRATCH BRUSH: A process using a soap solution with a soft, brass, rotating brush for restoring the lustre to a satin-finished, plated instrument.

SEAT: A term similar to Cover*. To seat a pad means to level it so that all sides touch evenly on the tone hole rim.

SET SCREW: A tiny screw inserted in a post* at a ninety degree angle to a pivot screw to lock it in place.

SHIM: A thin, paper or metal strip which is placed between two instrument parts to remove looseness. Paper washers* are also called shims.

SILENCER SKINS: Fish skins* that are placed on the ends of clarinet levers* to reduce the key noise.

SILVER SOLDER: The use of a silver alloy for soldering broken keys or instrument parts where a strong connection is needed.

SLEEVE: A tube* that slips into or over another tube, or a tube that connects two parts of an instrument, making them as one.

SLIDE BOW: 1. The short U-shaped tubing that is soft-soldered* into the sleeves* of a tuning slide. 2. The curved tubing at the bottom end of the trombone hand slide*.

SLIDE CROOK: Same as Slide Bow.

SLIDE KNOB: Same as Bow Knob*.

SOAP BARK: A soap solution used with water when scratch brushing*.

SOCKET: A recessed (or "drilled out") area in instruments into which a protruding part of equal size is inserted. Specifically, the recessed joint on a woodwind instrument into which the tenon* is inserted.

SOFT SOLDER: The lead and tin alloy used in soldering broad surfaces together where stress is light.

SPATULA: The flat part of a woodwind key or lever* that is operated by the fingers.

SPOT LACQUER: A process used in some shops whereby a small lacquered area which has been burned by soldering, or worn off by wear, is polished and re-lacquered.

SPRING BLOCK: A small, metal, grooved part of a woodwind key or body that holds the needle or flat spring in place when the key is in proper position.

SPRING CLAMP: A scissor-like clamp which holds a woodwind pad against the tone hole* for creating a firm seat* or ring on the pad.

SPRING HOOK: A device resembling a crochet needle that has a hook and groove on one end for attaching needle springs to the spring block*.

STACK: A group of keys operated by one hand—such as the

G, A, B♭, C keys (upper stack) operated by the left hand on saxophones — usually connected by one long hinge rod*.

STEM: The rod, or rod-like projection, on pistons* and rotary valves*.

STOCKINGS: The "swelled" portion at the bottom of the inner slide tubings on trombones which forms the main bearing surface for the hand slide*.

STOP PLATE: The flat plate attached to rotary valve* casings. This plate holds the cork bumpers*.

STRAPPING: Using a coarse, abrasive polish in a ragging* motion to eliminate file marks, scratches, and pits from brass instruments.

STRAP RING: The ring on an instrument to which a back strap, neck strap, or seat strap is attached for holding the instrument while playing.

STRIP: To remove old lacquer from an instrument. Other terms associated with strip are "hot," "cold," "lye," "tank," etc.

SWEDGE: The term used by repairmen to denote the stretching, lengthening, or tightening of keys, hinge rods, and hinge tubings to prevent loose action.

TABLE KEY: A woodwind key with a broad, flat surface for operating the key (low C, D♯, C♯, B, and B♭ on saxophones).

TAP: A screw-like tool for making threads inside a hole.

TEETER: A see-saw or teeter-totter key that is operated by the first finger (left hand) when using the alternate, high F fingering on saxophones.

TENON: The protruding end of an instrument section that fits into a socket* or tenon receiver*.

TENON CAP: 1. The cap placed on woodwind tenons* to protect them from chipping and collecting dirt while in the case. 2. A metal cap that is permanently fitted to the worn or chipped tenon*.

TENON RECEIVER: Same as Socket*.

TENSION RODS: The threaded rods on percussions that are utilized for tightening drum heads.

THROAT: The smallest diameter of a brass mouthpiece that regulates the air flow.

THUMB HOOK: A hook, normally soldered on the body of a saxophone, which enables the player to keep a steady right-hand position on the keys .

THUMB REST: A metal angle attached to clarinet and oboe bodies which gives the player a means of supporting the weight of the instruments and of keeping proper right hand placement.

THUMB RING: 1. The ring on altos, baritones, tubas, and sousaphones that assists the player in maintaining proper right-hand placement. 2. A ring attached to the first valve tuning slide on some cornets and trumpets that enables the player to move the slide for proper intonation.

THUMB SADDLE: Same purpose as a thumb ring (Number 2), except that it is in a U or saddle shape.

TONE HOLE: The hole in woodwind instruments which is covered by the fingers or pads.

TRIPOLI: A polishing compound used for rough buffing*.

TUBE: Any hollow, round cylinder or sleeve* used in brass instrument construction. Also used for tone holes (thumb and octave) on woodwinds.

TUNING BIT: A tapered sleeve*, fitting into the mouthpiece receiver*, which lengthens the mouthpipe* for proper pitch.

TUNING CORK: The cork in the head joint* of a flute or piccolo that determines its tuning pitch.

TUNING OIL: A thick oil used in lining tone holes on a wooden instrument to lower the pitch.

TURNBUTTON: Usually a movable, velvet-covered slat fastened by a screw. This slat holds the instrument or its parts in place inside the case.

VALVE CAP: The washer-like cap that screws into, or over, a piston* or rotary valve* casing. A valve cap is often erroneously confused with a finger button*.

VALVE GUIDE: The small metal or plastic tab attached to the side of a piston*, or one of several washer-like devices with a protruding tab which operates inside the groove in a valve casing, thereby keeping the valve ports in proper alignment.

VALVE STEM: A short rod which is screwed into the piston*, and into which the finger button* is screwed.

WHISPER KEY: The small key on a bassoon which seats* on the nib*.

YOKE: A U-shaped metal piece which, with the help of a screw or an axle, forms the stationary pivot point of a water key or valve trigger, etc.

Bibliography

REPAIR MANUALS

Brand, Erick D. *Band Instrument Repairing Manual.* Elkhart, Indiana: Erick D. Brand, 1946.

Nilles, Raymond J. *Basic Repair Handbook for Musical Instruments.* Fullerton, California: F. E. Olds & Son, 1959.

Tiede, Clayton H. *The Practical Band Instrument Repair Manual.* Dubuque, Iowa: Wm. C. Brown Company Publishers, 1962.

CARE AND MAINTENANCE PAMPHLETS

Conn Corporation. *How to Care for Your Instrument.* Elkhart, Indiana: C. G. Conn Ltd., 1942.

Hovey, Nilo W. *Selmer Band Manual.* Elkhart, Indiana: H. & A. Selmer, Inc., 1955.

King Musical Instruments. *How to Care for Your Instrument. Instruction Guide for Brass Instruments.* Eastlake, Ohio: King Musical Instruments, Division of the Seeburg Corporation, (N. D.).

_____*How to Care for Your Instrument. Instruction Guide for Trombones.* Eastlake, Ohio: King Musical Instruments, Division of the Seeburg Corporation, (N. D.).

_____*How to Care for Your Instrument. Instruction Guide for Woodwinds.* Eastlake, Ohio: King Musical Instruments, Division of the Seeburg Corporation, (N. D.).

Lehman, Paul R. *Teacher's Guide to the Oboe.* Elkhart, Indiana: H. & A. Selmer, Inc., 1965.

Pascucci, Vito. *Care and Minor Repairs of the Clarinet for Band Directors.* Kenosha, Wisconsin: G. Leblanc Corporation, 1959.

Pence, Homer. *Teacher's Guide to the Bassoon.* Elkhart, Indiana: H. & A. Selmer, Inc., 1963.

Weisshaar, Otto H. *Preventive Maintenance of Musical Instruments.* Rockville Centre, New York: Belwin, Inc., 1966.

REPAIR CHAPTERS IN TEXTBOOKS

Rogers, Charles C. "Instrument Repair and Maintenance," *The Band Director's Guide.* Written and edited by Kenneth L. Neidig. Englewood Cliffs, New Jersey: Prentice-Hall, Inc., 1964.

Richtmeyer, Lorin. "The Care and Repair of Instruments," *Music Education for Teen-Agers.* Second edition. William Raymond Sur and Charles Francis Schuller. New York: Harper & Row, Publishers, 1966.

REPAIR SUPPLY CATALOGS

Ed Myers Company, 3022 Pacific Street, Omaha, Nebraska 68105

Erick Brand, Elkhart, Indiana 46514

Feree's Band Instrument Tools and Supplies, 110 Calhoun Street, P.O. Box 259, Battle Creek, Michigan 49016

Appendix

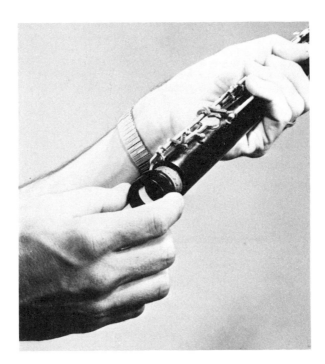

FIGURE 94
The tenon cap

FIGURE 95
The tapered trumpet mandrel

FIGURE 96
The tapered trombone mandrel

Index

NOTES

NOTES

NOTES

NOTES

NOTES

NOTES